Educating Children Without Housing

A Primer on Legal Requirements and Implementation Strategies for Educators, Advocates and Policymakers

pursuant to the
McKinney-Vento Homeless Assistance Act

Fourth Edition

Prepared by
Lisa M. Coleman
National Law Center on Homelessness & Poverty

Barbara J. Duffield
National Association for the Education of Homeless Children and Youth

Laurene M. Heybach
Law Project, Chicago Coalition for the Homeless

Patricia F. Julianelle
National Association for the Education of Homeless Children and Youth

Edited by
Amy E. Horton-Newell
ABA Commission on Homelessness & Poverty

Casey Trupin
Columbia Legal Services

**Defending Liberty
Pursuing Justice**

Commission on Homelessness & Poverty

The views expressed herein have not been approved by the House of Delegates or the Board of Governors of the American Bar Association and, accordingly, should not be construed as representing the policy of the American Bar Association. Nothing contained in this book is to be considered as the rendering of legal advice for specific cases, and readers are responsible for obtaining such advice from their own legal counsel.

Copyright © 2014 American Bar Association. All rights reserved. No part of this publication may be reproduced, stored in a retrieval system, or transmitted in any form or by any means, electronic, mechanical, photocopying, recording, or otherwise, without the prior written permission of the publisher. For permission contact the ABA Copyrights & Contracts Department, *copyright@americanbar.org* or via fax at (312) 988-6030.

Produced by the American Bar Association Commission on Homelessness and Poverty.

Printed in the United States of America.

ISBN: 978-1-62722-499-4
ISBN: 978-1-62722-500-7

Discounts are available for books ordered in bulk. For more information, contact the ABA Service Center at 1-800-285-2221.

http://apps.americanbar.org/abastore

CONTENTS

Chapter I

Chapter II

Chapter III

Chapter IV

Chapter V

Chapter VI

Chapter VII

Chapter VIII

CHAPTER IX

CHAPTER X

Chapter XI

Chapter XII

Chapter XIII

Endnotes

ABOUT THE AUTHORS AND EDITORS

Lisa M. Coleman, J.D.

Lisa M. Coleman serves as an education attorney at the National Law Center on Homelessness and Poverty. Lisa works closely with the Director of Children's Rights Programs to shape and implement programming to protect and enhance the education rights of homeless and unaccompanied children and youth. Additionally, Lisa provides technical assistance to legal services providers, advocates, government officials, and individuals across the country, and engages in impact litigation related to the education of homeless youth. Prior to joining the Law Center, Lisa served as a law fellow in the Educational Opportunities Project at the Lawyers' Committee for Civil Rights Under Law where she engaged in impact litigation and policy advocacy strategies to ensure underrepresented children and youth were provided equal access to a quality public school education. Lisa has also served at the Children's Defense Fund where she utilized policy advocacy tools to reduce disproportionate minority contact with the juvenile justice system and developed best practices for implementing appropriate gendered-responses for high-needs youth. Lisa received her J.D. from the American University Washington College of Law.

Barbara J. Duffield

Barbara J. Duffield is the Policy Director for the National Association for the Education of Homeless Children and Youth, where she advocates for effective policies and programs at the federal, state, and local levels. Barbara conducts trainings around the United States for school districts, community organizations, and local, state, and national groups to assist in the implementation of the McKinney-Vento Homeless Assistance Act. In addition, she serves on the Advisory Committee for the LeTendre Education Fund for Homeless Children. She began working on homeless issues as a tutor for children in Washington, DC in 1990. She subsequently joined the National Coalition for the Homeless where she served as Director of Education from 1994-2003. Barbara received her bachelors degree in Political Science *summa cum laude* from the University of Michigan.

Laurene M. Heybach, J.D.

Laurene M. Heybach is an attorney and Director of the Law Project of the Chicago Coalition for the Homeless. She received the Sandra Neese Lifetime Achievement Award from the National Association of State Coordinators of Education for Homeless Children and Youth in 1998 for her work on behalf of children experiencing homelessness. A 1978 graduate of Marquette University Law School, she has been a civil rights lawyer for thirty-five years and has worked on homelessness for twenty-four years. During the last twenty years her work has focused on the legal needs of children and families and particularly the needs of homeless families and youth. In conjunction with her staff, she has secured important legislative and policy changes in Illinois on behalf of homeless students as well as provided legal representation for hundreds of affected children. She has successfully brought litigation against school districts in Chicago and the surrounding suburbs on behalf of families, youth, and children experiencing homelessness to secure the rights afforded by the McKinney-Vento Act. The Law Project provides extensive community outreach to homeless families and offers training, training materials, and advice to professionals throughout Illinois.

Amy E. Horton-Newell, J.D.

Amy E. Horton-Newell has served as the Director of the Commission on Homelessness & Poverty at the American Bar Association since 2001. Amy is also the Director of the ABA Coordinating Committee on Veterans Benefits & Services. She coordinates ABA policy development and programming related to the special legal needs of people experiencing homelessness and poverty. On behalf of the Association, Amy collaborates with national, state and local advocacy groups, associations, and government agencies to address issues related to homelessness and poverty. From 2003 through 2011 Amy served on the Board of Directors for the Montgomery County Coalition for the Homeless in Maryland. Since 2011, she has served on the Montgomery County Continuum of Care as well as on the Planning Committee for the annual Montgomery County Homeless Resource Day. Amy received a Bachelor of Arts in Spanish from the University of Maryland, College Park, where she was elected to Phi Beta Kappa. She graduated from the University of Maryland School of Law where she focused on poverty law and street outreach, and was admitted to the Maryland Bar in 2000.

Patricia F. Julianelle, J.D.

Patricia F. Julianelle is Legal Director of the National Association for the Education of Homeless Children and Youth. She also works as an independent Legal Consultant for state and local governments and non-profit organizations, including: WA Office of Superintendent of Public Instruction (where she directed the State's Education for Homeless Children and Youth Program); the University of Texas; CA Homeless Youth Project; National Center for Homeless Education; and National Disabilities Rights Network. Patricia advises attorneys, educators and policymakers across the country on the rights of children and youth experiencing homelessness and works to enforce those rights through direct advocacy, education and outreach, and legislative advocacy. She travels extensively conducting workshops on the rights of children and youth at conferences across the nation, and her writing has been published in academic journals such as the *Children's Legal Rights Journal, Journal of Poverty Law and Policy, Seattle Journal for Social Justice,* and *Journal of Negro Education.* She co-authored two books. Patricia graduated from Yale University and received her J.D. *summa cum laude* from Northwestern School of Law of Lewis & Clark College. Patricia's commitment to advocating for youth's education arises from her experiences assisting juvenile public defenders, representing indigent families as a special education attorney, and experiencing urban education first-hand as an assistant high school teacher in Washington, DC and Portland, OR.

Casey Trupin, J.D.

Casey Trupin is the Coordinating Attorney for the Children and Youth Project at Columbia Legal Services in Seattle, where he advocates for at-risk, homeless and foster youth. Trupin has served as counsel to thousands of foster youth and homeless adults in litigation and worked on state and federal legislation designed to improve services to low-income children, youth and adults in Washington State and nationwide. Trupin is Co-Chair of the Children's Rights Litigation Committee of the American Bar Association (ABA) and is a Special Advisor to the ABA's Commission on Homelessness and Poverty, which he chaired from 2006-09. Trupin co-teaches the Legislative Advocacy Clinic at the University of Washington School of Law, and previously taught Street Law. Trupin has authored or edited numerous books and articles on at-risk, homeless and foster children, including *Educating Children without Housing: A Primer on Legal Requirements and Implementation Strategies for Educators, Advocates and Policymakers* (3d Ed.) (ABA, 2009). In 1997, Trupin co-founded Street Youth Legal Advocates of Washington (SYLAW), and went on to direct the program until 2005. From 2005-2006, Trupin worked on federal child welfare policy as Counsel for Special Projects at the Center for Law and Social Policy (CLASP) in Washington, D.C. Trupin has received national recognition for his work, including the ABA's Child Advocacy Award—Distinguished Lawyer (2011), the National Network for Youth Advocacy Spirit Award (2010), and the Congressional Angel in Adoption Award (2005). From 2006-12, Trupin served as the Inaugural Chair of the William H. Gates Public Service Law Program at the University of Washington School of Law, from which he graduated with honors in 1999.

ACKNOWLEDGMENTS

The American Bar Association Commission on Homelessness and Poverty thanks the authors for preparing this book and for their dedication to advocacy on behalf of children and youth experiencing homelessness as well as those in the foster care system. The authors and editors would like to acknowledge U.S. Senator Patty Murray (WA) and former U.S. Representative Judy Biggert (IL). Senator Murray and Representative Biggert have long served as champions for homeless students in the U.S. Congress. Representative Biggert and Senator Murray have worked to ensure that the nation's policies furthered the education of homeless students. Their leadership has helped to raise the visibility of this often-invisible population.

The Commission also thanks Kristin Kelly of the ABA Center on Children and the Law for drafting the sections related to children and youth in foster care, as well as Francine Hahn for drafting the sections related to early childhood education. Finally, the Commission thanks Tom Bolt, a Commission member and attorney practicing in St. Thomas, USVI, for his generous contribution in support of publishing this book.

ABOUT THE ABA COMMISSION ON HOMELESSNESS & POVERTY

The ABA Commission on Homelessness & Poverty is committed to educating the bar and the public about homelessness and poverty and the ways in which the legal community and advocates can assist those in need. In 2002, the Commission launched an initiative focused on the special legal needs of homeless children and youth, beginning with the publication of the first edition of *Educating Children Without Housing*. Since 2002, thousands of books have been distributed at free trainings, and several thousand more have been purchased in bulk quantities by state and local departments of education across the country.

Building on the success of its 2009 publication *Runaway and Homeless Youth and the Law: Model State Statutes*, the Commission has developed a set of advocacy resources and facilitated learning opportunities for the legal community and organizations and individuals working with homeless youth. The initiative features: guidance for states on model statutes pertaining to homeless youth; training sessions for lawyers; guidance on effective case law addressing the legal issues related to homeless youth; and articles on homeless youth and the law for publication in peer-reviewed publications and on appropriate organization Web sites.

Casey Trupin, an attorney at Columbia Legal Services in Seattle, WA, former Commission Chair, and Special Advisor for the Commission's Homeless Children & Youth Initiative, coordinates the Commission's technical assistance efforts. Numerous states have benefited from the advice provided through the initiative—advice which has helped bring about more effective laws, practices and policies for homeless youth.

For more information about the Commission, please contact the Commission Director, Amy Horton-Newell, at (202) 662-1693 or *Amy.Hortonnewell@americanbar.org.*

INTRODUCTION

The McKinney-Vento Homeless Assistance Act

The McKinney-Vento Homeless Assistance Act was enacted in 1987 as the first federal legislation intended to comprehensively combat homelessness. Title VII-B of the Act created the Education for Homeless Children and Youth Program, which authorized the appropriation of federal funds to states to ensure that children and youth experiencing homelessness receive a free, appropriate public education.[1] The Act strives to facilitate academic success for students experiencing homelessness by giving students the right to remain in one school despite their residential mobility and guaranteeing access to all appropriate educational opportunities and services. The Act also aims to eliminate the barriers that can delay or prevent a homeless student's access to public education. These barriers include proof of residency requirements, records requirements (including school records, birth certificates, and immunization and other medical records), guardianship requirements, and lack of transportation to school.

The Education of Homeless Children and Youth (EHCY) Program of the McKinney-Vento Homeless Assistance Act was reauthorized in January 2002 through the enactment of the No Child Left Behind Act.

The education provisions of the McKinney-Vento Act originated in policies and practices that proved successful at the local and state levels. The Act draws on the insight and experience of frontline educators, service providers, and advocates who strive to ensure that the educational needs of homeless students are met. The Act has widespread support among educators who work with children and youth in homeless situations. When implemented correctly, the McKinney-Vento provisions reflect strategies that have been shown to enhance students' academic and social growth and at the same time permit schools to benefit from the increased test scores and other achievements that are the result of educational continuity. Since the Act's reauthorization in 2002, notable progress has been made. A Department of Education report to Congress highlighted some of the accomplishments of the McKinney-Vento Act's EHCY program:

States and local educational agencies (LEAs) have generally made significant progress in reducing the barriers that homeless children and youth face in enrolling, attending, and succeeding in school. The legislation has prompted States and LEAs to focus more on the needs of homeless students and has helped facilitate the expansion of local support networks to meet those needs. More recently, McKinney-Vento has been an invaluable tool for assisting students who were left homeless by Hurricanes Katrina and Rita. Although the appropriation levels for this program are relatively small, the impact of the program has been very widespread.[2]

In addition, federal data from school districts with McKinney-Vento subgrants indicate that the number of homeless students included in state testing is increasing and that academic performance in reading and math is improving. However, the same federal data also reveal that many barriers persist, most notably transportation, records and other enrollment barriers, and general lack of awareness about the provisions of the law. Much work remains to be done toward ensuring that all students experiencing homelessness enroll, attend, and succeed in school.

The suggested implementation strategies in this book come from best practices—tried and true policies and techniques used by the frontline personnel in school buildings, by visionary school districts, and by judicious state administrators across the country. In this revised edition, we have included additional strategies designed to assist communities to exceed compliance and move toward greater commitment—to embody not only the letter but also the spirit of the law. Other additions include expanded sections on definitions, preschool children, and unaccompanied youth, and insights on application of the Act in response to disasters, as well as new chapters on the 2004 amendments to the Individuals with Disabilities Education Act and students involved in the child welfare system.

When the principles of access are denied to our most fragile group of citizens—our children and youth—the ABA's voice has been clear. The ABA Commission on Homelessness and Poverty has long fought for more inclusion of, and services to, homeless children and youth. As part of its initiative on Homeless Children and Youth, in 2009, the Commission released *Runaway and Homeless Youth and the Law: Model State Statutes*, to assist advocates and policymakers to improve their policies that relate to this population. Over the years, the Commission has consulted with states and internationally on how to better care for these children and youth, working not only with lawyers, but school personnel, social workers, and program administrators, as well. In this vein, we are pleased to present the fourth edition of this publication, on behalf of homeless children and youth, in order to better ensure that they do not suffer the consequences of homelessness in their adult lives.

CHAPTER 1

Issues of Homelessness and Education: Causes and Consequences

Homelessness is a lack of permanent housing resulting from extreme poverty and/or unsafe or unstable living environments (e.g., conditions of domestic violence, child abuse and neglect, or natural or other disasters). In the 2011-2012 school year, 1,168,354 homeless children and youth were enrolled in public schools.[3] This is a 72 percent increase from the 2006-2007 school year, and demonstrates the lingering impact of the economic recession and foreclosure crisis on homelessness.[4]

Two trends are largely responsible for the rise in family and youth homelessness over the past several decades: a growing shortage of affordable rental housing and a simultaneous increase in severe poverty. The mean income of families experiencing homelessness is less than half the poverty line.[5] There is a rising gap between income and housing costs for low-income individuals. For example, a full-time minimum wage worker cannot afford the fair market rent for housing in any jurisdiction within the United States.[6]

Despite the apparent need for affordable housing, the supply continues to dwindle. Between 2007 and 2011, the number of renter households with extremely low incomes (less than 30 percent of area medians) increased by 2.5 million. Over the same period, the number of available housing units that households at this income level could afford to rent declined by 135,000. As a result, the gap between the supply of affordable housing and demand from extremely low income renters doubled in just four years to 5.3 million units.[7] The lack of affordable housing has resulted in an increase in the number of people who become homeless. A 2013 survey of 25 U.S. cities found that shelters in 71 percent of the survey cities must turn away homeless families with children, and half of the survey cities expect the number of homeless families to increase over the next year.[8]

Unaccompanied youth include young people who have run away from or been thrown out of their home or been abandoned by their parents. The primary causes of homelessness among unaccompanied youth are physical and sexual abuse by a parent or guardian, neglect, parental substance abuse, and extreme family conflict. It is estimated that between 1.6 and 1.7 million youth run away or are forced to leave home each year.[9]

Decades of research illustrates how homelessness has a devastating impact on a child's education, health, and general well-being. In addition to enrollment problems, the high mobility associated with homelessness disrupts the student's education significantly. Although children and youth who experience homelessness represent the full range of academic talents and abilities, frequent residential moves—often as a result of limits on the length of shelter stays or unstable living arrangements—also put them at risk of falling behind in school. According to the Institute for Children and Poverty, homeless children are nine times more likely to repeat a grade, three times more likely to drop out of school, and more likely to be placed in special education programs than their housed peers.[10] Homelessness is associated with increased rates of hunger, as well as chronic and acute illnesses that may impede learning by causing absences and curtailing children's ability to concentrate on school work.

CHAPTER 11

Who is Eligible for Protections and Services under the McKinney-Vento Act? Issues of Definitions

Children and youth experiencing homelessness often do not fit society's stereotypical images of people who are homeless. The average family experiencing homelessness is headed by a single mother in her late 20s with two children, at least one of whom is under the age of six.[11] In addition, emergency shelters in urban and suburban areas cannot meet the rising need for temporary housing required by families, turning away requests for emergency shelter. Many shelters place eligibility restrictions on families and youth; for example, many shelters do not admit families with adolescent boys, or unaccompanied minors. Rural areas also have people experiencing homelessness, though they often have no shelters at all.[12] Families and youth may not have enough money to stay at a motel, or they may leave their homes in crisis, fleeing to the first available location.

As a result of the lack of shelter, most students in homeless situations share housing with others or stay in motels or other temporary facilities. These situations are precarious, damaging, crowded, and unstable, leading to extraordinary rates of mobility. According to federal data, of the children and youth identified as homeless and enrolled in public schools in the 2011-2012 school year, only 15 percent lived in shelters. Seventy-five percent lived doubled-up with other family members or friends, 6 percent lived in motels, and the remainder lived in unsheltered locations.[13] Despite their large numbers, children and youth not living in shelters may not immediately be recognized as homeless and are thus sometimes denied protections and services which the McKinney-Vento Act provides. Therefore, the Act contains a specific definition of homelessness that includes clarification of the broad array of inadequate living situations. This definition can help educators, families, and youth understand who is entitled to the Act's protections.

The definition of homelessness in the education subtitle of the McKinney-Vento Act is different from the definition of homelessness used by the U.S. Department of Housing and Urban Development (HUD). The current HUD definition of homelessness, which was changed in 2009, is limited to people who are living on the streets or who are staying in shelters, those who can stay in motels or doubled-up situations for 14 days or less, those fleeing or attempting to flee domestic violence or other life-threatening situations, and those in long-term, highly mobile homeless situations. Schools, however, are legally responsible for serving children and youth included in the broader definition of homelessness included in the education subtitle. Assisting all community agencies to understand the education definition of homelessness is an important step toward ensuring that children and youth living in the full range of homeless situations covered by the Act receive the support they need to enroll, attend, and succeed in school.

What the McKinney-Vento Act Says:

For the purposes of this subtitle, the term 'homeless child and youth'

■ *means individuals who lack a fixed, regular, and adequate nighttime residence (within the meaning of section 103(a)(1)); and*

■ *includes –*

   (i) children and youth who lack a fixed, regular, and adequate nighttime residence, and includes children and youth who are sharing the housing of other persons due to loss of housing, economic hardship, or a similar reason; are living in motels, hotels, trailer parks, or camping grounds due to lack of alternative adequate accommodations; are living in emergency or transitional shelters; are abandoned in hospitals; or are awaiting foster care placement;

   (ii) children and youth who have a primary nighttime residence that is a private or public place not designed for or ordinarily used as a regular sleeping accommodation for human beings (within the meaning of section 103(a)(2)(C));

   (iii) children and youth who are living in cars, parks, public spaces, abandoned buildings, substandard housing, bus or train stations, or similar settings; and

   (iv) migratory children (as such term is defined in section 1309 of the Elementary and Secondary Education Act of 1965) who qualify as homeless for the purposes of this subtitle because the children are living in circumstances described in clauses (i) through (iii).

■ *The term unaccompanied youth includes youth in homeless situations who are not in the physical custody of a parent or guardian.*

CHAPTER III

Who Has Primary Responsibility for Implementing the McKinney-Vento Act? State and Local Personnel

The high mobility associated with homelessness can have severe educational consequences. Families and youth who are homeless are often forced to move frequently due to limits on length of shelter stays, their search for safe and affordable housing or employment, or to escape unsafe living situations. All too often, children in homeless situations change schools because shelters or other temporary accommodations are not located in their school district and/or they lack transportation to continue attending class at their same school—despite federal educational protections that entitle them to stay in the same school and to receive transportation to and from that school. School transfers have a well-documented negative effect on academic achievement, as do lack of quiet, safe places to do homework, lack of school supplies, and lack of food.[14]

In addition to mobility, homeless children and youth face a number of barriers to accessing an appropriate education, and as a result, they are often precluded from achieving academic success. School policies and practices, as well as lack of awareness about homelessness and federal education law, may ultimately create barriers to the free and appropriate education of students in homeless situations. For example, residency requirements, guardianship requirements, delays in transfer of school records, lack of transportation, and records requirements may prevent homeless students from enrolling in school. Even after they enroll in school, students in homeless situations still face barriers to regular attendance, such as higher rates of chronic and acute illnesses, lack of transportation, residential mobility, and the many severe challenges of surviving without a place to call home.

In response to these barriers, Congress passed Subtitle VII-B of the McKinney-Vento Homeless Assistance Act, Education for Homeless Children and Youth. Originally enacted in 1987, the statute was reauthorized as part of the No Child Left Behind Act in January 2002. The McKinney-Vento Act's broad mandate is to eliminate barriers to school success for children who are homeless so that they may meet the same challenging academic standards as all other children. It incorporates many policies and practices that have proven successful at the local and state levels. The McKinney-Vento Act is an essential part of the overall mission of the No Child Left Behind Act: to ensure that every child in the United States is successful in school, and to close the achievement gap between disadvantaged students and their more fortunate peers.

Responsibilities for implementing the McKinney-Vento Act are shared at the federal, state, and local level. This booklet is primarily geared to local school personnel; therefore, it provides more detailed information about state and local responsibilities. More information about the federal role is detailed in the statute and in the regulations, which can be found at *center.serve.org/nche/legis/mv.php.*

Office of the State Coordinator and State Educational Agency Responsibilities

The McKinney-Vento Act requires that every state educational agency (SEA) establish an Office of State Coordinator for the Education of Homeless Children and Youth. This office is charged with critical responsibilities with respect to the implementation of the Act, including providing technical assistance, resources, coordination, data collection, and overseeing compliance for all local educational agencies (LEA) in the state.

What the Act Says:

■ *Every SEA must establish an Office of State Coordinator for the Education of Homeless Children and Youth. The responsibilities of this office include the following:*

1. *Gathering information on the extent of homelessness among children and youth and their educational needs and progress;*

2. *Developing and carrying out a state plan for the education of homeless students;*

3. *Facilitating coordination between state education and state social service agencies;*

4. *Coordinating and collaborating with educators, including preschool programs; administrators of homeless service programs, including family and runaway and homeless youth programs; local educational agency liaisons; and community organizations representing homeless children and youth; and*

5. *Providing technical assistance to all LEAs, in coordination with LEA liaisons, to ensure compliance with the Act.*

■ *SEAs must implement strategies to address problems resulting from enrollment delays caused by immunization and medical records requirements, residency requirements, lack of birth certificates, school records or other documentation, guardianship issues, or uniform or dress code requirements.*

■ *SEAs and LEAs must develop, review, and revise their policies to remove barriers to the enrollment and retention of children and youth in homeless situations.*

A list of state coordinators may be found on the Web site of the National Center for Homeless Education at *center.serve.org/nche/states/state_resources.php.*

Local Educational Agency Liaisons and Local Educational Agency Responsibilities

Liaisons are LEA staff responsible for ensuring the identification, school enrollment, attendance, and opportunities for academic success of students in homeless situations. Some of these activities may be accomplished by the liaison himself or herself, while others are accomplished by coordinating the efforts of other staff and community partners. National evaluations indicate that liaisons are a necessary common denominator for successful district efforts to identify and support students experiencing homelessness. Therefore, the McKinney-Vento Act requires every LEA to designate a liaison for students who are homeless and specifies their legal responsibilities. The U.S. Department of Education's 2006 Report to Congress on the implementation of the EHCY Program describes the demonstrated benefits of having a local liaison in every school district, including increased identification of homeless children and youth, increased service provision, better coordination among school district programs, increased awareness of homeless children and youth among school and school district staff, and increased awareness of issues related to homeless education in the community. By linking students and their families to school and community services, liaisons play a critical role in stabilizing students and promoting academic achievement at the individual, school, and district level.

Throughout all school districts, there are numerous and differing programs, departments, initiatives, and events. Early childhood, transportation, pupil support, truancy, special education, athletics, afterschool programs, and literacy are all examples. Each particular activity has its own objectives, staff, time frames, forms, and mechanisms for including students and families in the school community.

Because no McKinney-Vento liaison can be at the helm of every school program, it is critical that schools and personnel in any district bring these program staff together under district leadership to methodically plan how homeless students will be served and integrated into each of the activities. This can be done in the context of already existing structures such as annual school improvement planning, Title I planning activities, or multi-year strategic planning.

An overarching responsibility of LEAs is to assist homeless students in accessing all the district programs; to identify and remove barriers to the enrollment, attendance, and success of homeless students. District-wide and school planning should include a review of all programs and services, goals, and materials to ensure that the needs of homeless students have been carefully considered and are clearly addressed. For example, music or arts initiatives must address how homeless students will be included, provided instruments or materials and transported. Similarly, pre-enrollment programs should make provision for newer students who were unable to pre-enroll. In short, removing barriers is a district-wide, collaborative effort, not an isolated task for the liaison alone.

What the Act Says:

■ *Every LEA must designate an appropriate staff person as a liaison for students in homeless situations. This person may also be a coordinator for other Federal programs.*

■ *Liaisons must ensure that:*

1. *Children and youth in homeless situations are identified by school personnel and through coordination activities with other entities and agencies;*

2. *Students enroll in, and have full and equal opportunity to succeed in, the schools of the LEA;*

3. *Families, children, and youth receive educational services for which they are eligible, including Head Start, Even Start, and preschool programs administered by the LEA, as well as referrals to health, mental health, dental, and other appropriate services;*

4. *Parents or guardians are informed of educational and related opportunities available to their children and are provided with meaningful opportunities to participate in the education of their children;*

5. *Public notice of the educational rights of students in homeless situations is disseminated where children and youth receive services under the Act;*

6. *Enrollment disputes are mediated in accordance with the Enrollment Disputes section of the McKinney-Vento Act; and*

7. *Parents, guardians, and unaccompanied youth are fully informed of all transportation services, including to the school of origin, and are assisted in accessing transportation services.*

■ *Liaisons must assist children and youth who do not have immunizations, or immunization or other medical records, to obtain necessary immunizations, or immunization or other medical records.*

■ *Liaisons must help unaccompanied youth choose and enroll in a school, after considering the youth's wishes, and provide him or her with notice of the right to appeal an enrollment decision that is not their choice.*

■ *Liaisons must ensure that unaccompanied youth are immediately enrolled in school pending resolution of disputes that might arise over school enrollment or placement.*

■ *SEAs and LEAs must develop, review, and revise their policies to remove barriers to the enrollment and retention of students in homeless situations.*

■ *State coordinators and LEAs must inform school personnel, service providers, and advocates who work with families in homeless situations of the duties of the LEA homeless liaison.*

How Your School and District Can Implement the Act:

• LEA administrators should work with the Office of State Coordinator for the Education of Homeless Children and Youth to identify an appropriate staff person to serve as the LEA homeless liaison. This staff person should have sufficient time and authority to carry out the mandated responsibilities. Federal programs, such as Title I, Even Start, or Migrant Education, may be good offices to support this position. State programs for students in high-risk situations may also be appropriate. Larger districts should consider des-

Continued next page

ignating liaisons in each school to enable coordinated and effective response to student needs. This model has been critical to serving homeless students in Chicago's 600 schools.

- LEAs should create opportunities for the designated liaison to receive sufficient training including issues related to homelessness, legal responsibilities of the liaison, and key provisions of the McKinney-Vento Act. Materials such as Local Homeless Education Toolkit and other important resources are available on the Web site of the National Center for Homeless Education (NCHE) at *center.serve.org/nche/index.php.* See Chapter XIII for additional resources.

- Liaisons must disseminate posters, brochures, and other awareness materials explaining educational rights, programs, and related services, in schools and other locations where children and youth receive services (such as food banks, health clinics, shelters, transitional living programs for youth, street outreach teams, youth drop-in centers, motels, campgrounds, and public laundries). Posters for parents and for unaccompanied youth may be found on the NCHE Web site at *center.serve.org/nche/index.php.*

- Liaisons should ensure that all printed material, forms, websites, and social media pertinent to students and families sensitively reflect inclusion of homeless student needs. For example, general enrollment and registration materials, online applications, and any appeal for parent participation should be user-friendly for homeless families.

- Under the Child Nutrition and WIC Act of 2004, homeless students are automatically eligible for free meals and do not have to submit an application. Liaisons should submit the names of homeless students who would like to receive free school meals to the local school nutrition office. More information may be found on NAEHCY's Web site at *www.naehcy.org/educational-resources/food.*

- Liaisons should work closely with local directors of other school programs, such as Title I (see Chapter V), preschool, Special Education, Teen Parenting, Child Nutrition, Migrant Education, Neglected and Delinquent, Even Start, and Health Services to ensure that students who are homeless can access those services as needed.

- Liaisons should seek program support from public and private community organizations. Community organizations can often donate money, materials, and time to support the liaison's work.

- Liaisons should develop relationships with key school personnel, including administrators, principals, secretaries, registrars, teachers, counselors, social workers, transportation staff, athletic and extracurricular staff, food services staff, school nurses, and truancy officers. They should inform these personnel about the causes and consequences of homelessness, signs of homelessness, the duties of the liaison, the responsibilities of the school district, and the rights of students and families who are homeless.

- Liaisons should join local homeless task forces, homeless coalitions and their local homeless assistance Continuum of Care. A directory of state and local homeless coalitions may be found at the National Coalition for the Homeless Web site at *nationalhomeless.org/references/directory/*. These organizations can support the liaison's work and be important community partners.

- To identify and serve students who lose their housing in natural and other disasters, liaisons should collaborate with local representatives of disaster relief organizations such as the Federal Emergency Management Agency (FEMA), the Red Cross, the Salvation Army, and the National Voluntary Organizations Active in Disaster (NVOAD). Collaboration should focus on: building relationships and establishing quick, reliable communication systems with relief agency personnel prior to disasters occurring; training disaster relief agencies in the McKinney-Vento Act and sharing posters, brochures, and other awareness materials; developing information-sharing strategies; and integrating the school into community disaster planning, response, and recovery activities.

- Lists of social service referrals for school staff to utilize should be made widely available by LEAs and should include shelter and housing agencies, youth programs, domestic violence services, mental health providers, food resources, and legal aid programs.

- Liaisons should involve homeless parents and youth in implementing the LEA's duty to identify and revise policies and practices that act as barriers to homeless students.

CHAPTER IV

School Responsibilities and Implementation Strategies

Identification and Outreach to Families and Youth Experiencing Homelessness

The McKinney-Vento Act requires Local Educational Agencies (LEAs) to be proactive in identifying which children and youth are "homeless" within the broad definitions of the Act—including those homeless students who are attending school, as well as those who are not attending school. It is not sufficient for a school or LEA to passively await the enrollment of homeless students. Indeed, few families will appear before a clerk or principal and simply announce that they are "homeless." Many families are unaware, for example, that living doubled-up in a friend's or relative's home because they cannot afford their own home constitutes homelessness or that sharing information about their homelessness could result in getting additional services, such as transportation, from the school. Others, including adolescents experiencing homelessness, may feel deeply ashamed of their living situation and try to conceal it.

Therefore, specific steps must be taken to notify the school body and larger community, as well as the potential parents and students who may benefit from the Act, of the services and benefits to which they may be entitled. Eligible families, children, and youth must be identified so that the appropriate steps may be taken to ensure the enrollment, attendance, and success of those students. Certain populations (e.g., adolescents living on the street or for whom issues of sexual orientation and gender identity are critical) may require intensive and varying strategies to seek them out and ensure their enrollment. Preschool children experiencing homelessness also may be overlooked without special efforts to locate them.

1. Identification

There are two aspects to the obligation to "identify" homeless children and youth. One is simply to understand which students within the school may meet the definition of "homeless" so that each of them may be afforded full access to services and so that the school is able to obtain an accurate count of the number of students experiencing homelessness. The other is to locate potential students not currently within the school system who are homeless and school-age, to ensure that they are enrolled or rejoined to appropriate school programs. This second effort at identification is often referred to as "outreach." While it applies to all age groups, it has particular meaning for older youth who may have left or dropped out of school for a variety of reasons and preschool-age children who are not covered by compulsory education laws, but who may benefit greatly from early childhood education.

What the Act Says:

▨ *Each state must describe in its state plan the procedures for identification of homeless children and youth, including those who are separated from school.*

▨ *Special attention must be given to ensuring the enrollment and attendance of homeless children and youth who are not currently attending school.*

▨ *School personnel have the obligation to perform such identification.*

▨ *The LEA liaison must ensure that school personnel meet their duty to identify homeless children and youth, as well as to conduct additional identification through coordination with other entities and agencies.*

How Your School and District Can Implement the Act:

• Train staff at all levels to understand the definitions of homeless and to identify the subtle cues that suggest a student or parent may be experiencing homelessness. LEAs have found it very valuable to train personnel such as registrars, secretaries, school counselors, school social workers, school nurses, teachers, bus drivers, and cafeteria workers to recognize some of those cues.

• Create enrollment forms that capture housing information in a sensitive and confidential manner which will aid in identifying homeless living arrangements. Examples of such forms are available in the Local Homeless Liaison Toolkit on the Web site of the National Center on Homeless Education at *center.serve.org/nche/*. Using sensitive adapted language, an emergency contact form can be used by all schools upon enrollment in order to seek housing information.

• Utilize the LEA liaison, social workers, counselors, and attendance officers to coordinate with agencies and service providers within the community who are able to, or have the responsibility for, identifying homeless families and children (e.g., shelters, soup kitchens, food banks, street outreach teams, legal aid programs, drop-in centers, and public benefit, housing, and public health departments).

- Provide outreach materials and display posters where there is a frequent influx of low-income families and youth in high-risk situations, including motels and campgrounds.

- Using support staff who are able to leave the campus, provide special attention to children and youth not currently in school.

- Teachers can ask students to draw or write about where they live and examine the assignments for possible indicators of homelessness.

- Avoid using the word "homeless" in initial contacts with families, youth, or school personnel. The word often conjures up stereotypical images that may prevent proper identification.

- If a school district wishes to verify homelessness, it must not conduct any activities that would jeopardize circumstances of the enrolling family or youth. For example, the school district must not contact a landlord or enforcement authority where a family claims to be living doubled up, in the event that he or she does not know the family is there and occupancy limits exist. The confidentiality of the family and youth must be protected.

2. Notice

Knowledge is power. If a family experiencing homelessness lacks information about the rights of homeless children and youth, the child or youth may be prevented from remaining in a stable school setting with access to transportation, tutoring, or other services. Similarly, without the appropriate information, the larger community of child welfare agencies, community-based organizations, legal aid programs, libraries, and advocates who can direct children to the schools may fail to do so. Schools will continue to suffer unnecessarily high mobility rates and lower performance if families and assistance organizations remain ignorant of the educational rights of homeless students.

What the Act Says:

■ *The LEA liaison must ensure that public notice of the educational rights of homeless children and youth is disseminated in areas where those children and youth receive services, such as schools, shelters, and soup kitchens.*

■ *Parents and guardians experiencing homelessness must be informed of the education and related options available to their children and provided with meaningful opportunities to participate in their children's education.*

■ *Parents and guardians of homeless students and unaccompanied youth must be fully informed of their right to transportation services.*

How Your School and District Can Implement the Act:

- Create colorful and informative posters that clearly explain the rights and benefits for homeless students and consider adopting non-stigmatizing language to do so such as "students facing transition" or "students in temporary living situations;" post them prominently throughout schools and enlist community support in placing these posters throughout the community. Posters for parents and unaccompanied youth may be found on the NCHE Web site at *center.serve.org/nche/.*

- Create easy-to-read and informative brochures to distribute to all families in the school on a regular basis. These brochures should explain who is considered to be homeless, the availability of transportation and details about requesting it, information regarding the educational programs and services offered by the school, and the name and phone number of the LEA liaison. Additionally, distribute these brochures at shelters, libraries, child welfare agencies, public aid offices, community-based organizations, parks, bus stations, and food banks. Many written materials and posters are available through the NCHE. Posters and materials should also be available in languages other than English.

- Provide such a brochure to every person who seeks enrollment or information about enrollment in the school or the LEA.

- Request local television and radio stations to run public service announcements providing this information.

- Post information on the school and district Web sites.

Redetermining Homelessness

The McKinney-Vento Homeless Assistance Act requires schools to allow homeless students to remain at their schools of origin as long as they are considered homeless as defined in the Act. Students may remain in the school of origin until the end of any academic year in which they move into permanent housing. Schools may, but are not required to, redetermine the homeless status of children and youth to ensure that students are still eligible for McKinney-Vento services. Redetermination can occur annually or on an as-needed basis when homeless families experience changes in housing status or transportation needs. Schools should show sensitivity and respect to families and should make only reasonable requests when redetermining eligibility under the Act.

In Redetermining Eligibility under the Act, a School Should:

- Establish a written policy for the redetermination of homeless students under the Act. The school should distribute this policy and conduct trainings for homeless liaisons, school social workers, homeless families, and any other interested parties.

- Establish relationships with homeless families through the school's homeless liaisons or school social workers. Liaisons should contact the families informally throughout the year to check on their housing status and ensure that the school is meeting homeless students' needs.

- Provide information about McKinney-Vento services if families display homelessness indicators.

- Immediately enroll homeless students in the schools where they seek enrollment and allow students to attend classes as usual, even during the redetermination process. To determine that a student is no longer homeless, a school must confirm that the student has retained permanent housing.

- If a district determines that a student does not meet the requirements of the Act, it should provide the family with a written explanation of its decision as well as the family's right to appeal the decision. The homeless liaison should help the family complete the appeal and dispute resolution process. The school must continue

Continued next page

enrollment and transportation for the entirety of the dispute resolution process.

- Before transferring a student to a new school, a district should engage in an individualized feasibility determination by weighing factors such as the student's age, need for specialized education, safety, effect of commuting on the student's education, likely length of stay in current housing, and time remaining in the school year to determine the best school for the student.

To Remain in Compliance with the Act, a School Should *Not:*

- Remove students previously identified as homeless from the current year's enrollment.

- Disenroll students without first providing an explanation of the reasons for the change in status and a reasonable opportunity for the family to respond and/or appeal.

- Remove a student's information from school records.

- Tell students or families that they must disenroll or enroll immediately in a new school district.

- Automatically disenroll homeless students between school years.

- Automatically disenroll homeless students when they are progressing from a lower school to a higher school (elementary to middle or middle to high school).

These tactics are not in compliance with the Act, are harmful to homeless students and families, and are punishable by law. Schools should instead use practices, some of which are outlined above, that meet the requirements of the Act and meet the needs of the students they serve.

The following is a suggested timeline of best practices for redetermining the status of homeless students. It includes suggestions on checking in with homeless families throughout the year and other activities to ensure that students' needs are met.

First Day of School:

- Distribute Student Residency Questionnaire (SRQ) written in all major languages of the district. See sample SRQs at ***center.serve.org/ nche/downloads/residency_ques_eng.pdf.***

- Immediately enroll the student even if a family fails to return the SRQ.

First Month of School:

- Follow up if SRQ is not returned (homeless liaisons, school social workers).

- File returned SRQ in the student's cumulative records folder, making sure to maintain confidentiality of the student's information and homeless status.

- Create a centralized list of students eligible for McKinney-Vento each school year, which helps schools contact and check in with homeless students throughout the year.

- Schools with large homeless populations can divide this list among liaisons or school administrators so each liaison works with the same group of families throughout the school year.

Throughout the School Year:

- Watch for "red flags" of consistent truancy or absence from school, which may indicate housing or transportation issues.

- If a red flag exists, check in with the family informally to determine the student's housing status, and reassess transportation arrangements if needed.

Winter Break/Spring Break:

- Reach out informally to families by phone or in person.

- Inquire about housing status and ask whether the family plans to move during winter or spring break. To ensure stability, encourage families and youth to remain in the same school throughout the year.

- Determine whether the school met the student's needs during first semester.

- If the student's needs were not met, propose and implement improvements.

- Provide the student with a flyer of information about services and rights under McKinney-Vento. The flyer should be printed in all major languages.

Just Before or During Summer Break:

- Homeless liaisons or school social workers reach out informally to families by phone or in person.

- Ask whether the family plans to re-enroll in the same district next year or plans to transfer schools. Encourage families and youth to consider the harmful effects of school mobility in making any school transfer choice.

- Help the family complete re-registration or transfer processes as needed.

- If a student plans to transfer, complete a transfer SRQ to send to the new school.

- Schools may redetermine families' homeless status at this point in the year.

- Schools relying on 9-month employees, such as social workers, to complete the determination should conduct the Third Check-In before the school year ends rather than during summer break.

Stability and School Selection
1. School of Origin

Extensive research documents the negative effects of involuntary school transfers on a student's academic, social, and emotional development. Experts believe that it takes a child four to six months to recover academically after changing schools.[15] Highly mobile students have been found to have lower test scores and overall inferior academic performance than peers who do not change schools.[16] To avoid these negative results, the McKinney-Vento Act places great emphasis on keeping students stable in their schools. School districts that have embraced the Act's requirements have documented increased attendance and higher test scores among students who are homeless. The resulting educational stability enhances a student's academic and social growth, while permitting schools to benefit from the increased test scores and other achievements shown to result from student continuity.

What the Act Says:

▨ *"School of origin" is defined as the school that the child or youth attended when permanently housed or the school in which the child or youth was last enrolled.*

▨ *Local Educational Agencies (LEAs) must keep a student experiencing homelessness in his or her school of origin, to the extent feasible, unless it is against the parent's or guardian's wishes.*

▨ *The student may remain in the school of origin for the duration of homelessness. He or she may also stay in the school of origin until the end of any academic year in which he or she moves into permanent housing.*

▨ *The student may also enroll in any public school that students living in the same attendance area are eligible to attend. (See section 3 below regarding enrollment.)*

▨ *Schools must ensure equal access to educational programs and a full and equal opportunity to succeed. Therefore, other school options such as selective enrollment, charter, and specialized schools must be made available to homeless students on a non-discriminatory basis.*

▨ *If a student is sent to a school other than one requested by a parent or guardian, the district must provide a written explanation to the parent or guardian of its decision and of his/her right to appeal.*

▨ *LEA homeless liaisons must help unaccompanied youth choose and enroll in a school, after considering the youth's wishes, and provide the youth with notice of the right to appeal the liaison's decision.*

How Your School and District Can Implement the Act:

- Make sure families and unaccompanied youth know about the impact of school mobility and the right of the student to attend either the school of origin or the local school, and procedures for accessing other selective, charter, or specialized schools of the district as well as their right to transportation to the school of origin and immediate enrollment.

- Make sure all school staff handling enrollment issues are aware of the Act's provisions and work to implement stability.

- Develop clear, understandable forms to be used for written explanations of decisions and notification of the right to appeal.

Continued next page

- Make sure school staff understand the benefits of school stability, including registrars, counselors, teachers, and administrators.

- Make sure shelter providers and community agencies understand the benefits of school stability and develop policies that align with the Act to promote educational continuity.

- Consult this guide for making sound decisions about school selection: *center.serve.org/nche/downloads/dis/school_choice_checklist.pdf.*

2. Transportation

Transportation is essential to enable students to attend and remain in school. Poverty, mobility, and the unstable living situations facing homeless children and youth can make getting to and from school extremely challenging. Recognizing this significant barrier to attendance and success, the McKinney-Vento Act contains provisions requiring transportation for students experiencing homelessness. The U.S. Department of Education's 2006 Report to Congress notes that these provisions have increased school stability and limited the educational disruption that students experience when they lose their housing.[17] Similarly, an evaluation of a federal demonstration program in Washington State found that homeless children who received transportation to stay in their schools of origin scored higher on state assessments.[18]

What the Act Says:

■ *LEAs must provide transportation to and from the school of origin for students experiencing homelessness, at a custodial parent's or guardian's request.*

■ *For unaccompanied youth, LEAs must provide transportation to and from the school of origin at the LEA homeless liaison's request.*

■ *If the student's temporary residence and the school of origin are in the same LEA, that LEA must provide or arrange for transportation. If the student is living outside the school of origin's LEA, the LEA where the student is living and the school of origin's LEA must determine how to divide the responsibility and cost of providing transportation. If they cannot come to an agreement, they must share the responsibility and cost equally.*

In addition to providing transportation to the school of origin, LEAs must also provide students in homeless situations with other transportation services comparable to those provided to other students.

How Your School and District Can Implement the Act:

- Coordinate with local shelter and housing authorities and community-based organizations to house students near their schools of origin and to reduce shelter or housing moves.

- Ensure transportation services and arrangements are appropriate for a given student.

- Re-route school buses (including special education, magnet school, and other buses) and ensure that school buses travel to shelters, transitional living programs, and motels where students reside.

- Develop close ties among LEA homeless liaisons, school staff, and student transportation staff.

- Develop inter-district transportation agreements to coordinate inter-district transportation and avoid delays and disputes.

- Designate a district-level point of contact to arrange and coordinate transportation.

- Provide sensitivity training to bus drivers and arrange bus stops to keep students' living situations confidential.

- Provide passes for public transportation, including passes for caregivers when necessary.

- Collaborate with local public and nonprofit agencies and service providers to develop transportation plans or provide transportation.

- Take advantage of transportation systems used by public assistance agencies and coordinate with those agencies.

- Reimburse parents, guardians, or unaccompanied youth for gas if they are able to provide their own transportation.

- Obtain corporate or other sponsorship for transportation costs.

- For more implementation strategies, visit **center.serve.org/nche/ibt/sc_transport.php** for the National Center for Homeless Education's publications on transportation for children and youth in homeless situations.

3. Enrollment

Children and youth experiencing homelessness often lack the documents ordinarily required for school enrollment. Domestic violence, natural disasters, evictions, and unstable living situations can make it impossible for parents or unaccompanied youth to retain documents. Nonetheless, school is vitally important for children and youth in homeless situations. It may be their only opportunity to benefit from a stable environment, the normalcy of teacher and peer relations, academic stimulation, and reliable meals. Immediately enrolling students in homeless situations in school provides stability and avoids the personal, educational, and social trauma involved when children are separated from their school for days or weeks while documents are located.

What the Act Says:

■ *Schools must keep homeless students in their school of origin (to the extent feasible) or enroll them in any public school that students living in the same attendance area are eligible to attend. LEA liaisons must help unaccompanied youth choose and enroll in a school, after considering the youth's wishes. If a student is sent to a school other than one requested by a parent or guardian, the school must provide a written explanation of its decision and the right to appeal.*

■ *Students must be enrolled in school immediately, even if they do not have the required documents, such as school records, medical records, proof of residency, or other documents. "Enrolled" means attending classes and participating fully in school activities.*

■ *If a student has not had immunizations or does not have immunization or medical records, the liaison must immediately provide assistance in obtaining them, and the student must be enrolled in school in the interim.*

■ *Enrolling schools must obtain school records from the previous school, and students must be enrolled in school while records are being obtained. Schools must maintain records for students who are homeless so they are readily available.*

■ *SEAs and LEAs must develop, review, and revise their policies to remove barriers to the enrollment and retention of children and youth in homeless situations. SEAs and LEAs must find ways to address enrollment delays caused by immunization and medical records requirements, residency requirements, lack of birth certificates, school records or other documentation, guardianship issues, or uniform or dress code requirements.*

How Your School and District Can Implement the Act:

- Train all school enrollment staff, secretaries, school counselors, school social workers, and principals on the legal requirements for immediate enrollment.

- Make sure families and youth know about their right to attend either the school of origin or the local school, including rights to transportation to the school of origin and immediate enrollment.

- Review all LEA policies to make sure all barriers to enrollment and retention are removed. Pay particular attention to policies on enrollment procedures and requirements; school fees (which must be waived); transportation; access to selective enrollment, charter and specialized schools; evaluations for and placement in special education, English language learner services, gifted and talented programs, school meals, vocational and technical education, before and after school programs, and Title I programs; attendance and truancy; preschool; school discipline; and award and transfer of credits, among others.

- Develop statements of residency or other forms to replace typical proof of residency. Such forms should be carefully crafted so that they do not create further barriers or delay enrollment.

- Develop caregiver statements, enrollment forms for unaccompanied youth, and other forms to replace typical proof of guardianship. Again, such forms should be carefully crafted so that they do not create further barriers or delay enrollment.

- Establish immunization databases, school-based immunization clinics, or other opportunities for on-site immunizations.

- Collaborate with community-based or public agencies to provide appropriate clothing or school uniforms, and work to standardize school uniforms within a district and among neighboring districts.

- Accept school records directly from families and youth.

- Develop clear, understandable forms to be used for written explanations of decisions and notification of the right to appeal.

- Visit the Web site of the National Center for Homeless Education at

Continued next page

center.serve.org/nche/ibt/sc_enroll.php for numerous enrollment resources, including a "ready reference" desktop booklet.

- To help provide a smooth transition for teachers and students:

  1. Contact previous teachers and develop short educational assessments to facilitate placing students immediately if academic records are not readily available;

  2. Expeditiously follow up on any special education referrals or services;

  3. Provide necessary remediation and tutoring;

  4. Have custodial parents and students meet with counselors shortly after enrollment;

  5. Identify faculty and peer mentors/buddies;

  6. Start a "New Students" club;

  7. Take time to talk to and welcome students individually;

  8. Establish school-level and classroom-level routines for incoming and departing transfers;

  9. Get to know new students with an initial questionnaire or journal assignment;

  10. Introduce new students to the class;

  11. Keep a short, simple written list of classroom rules and procedures;

  12. Make sure the students have a chance to have a class job/role and to participate in extracurricular activities; and

  13. Start and maintain a portfolio of class work for the students to take with them when leaving the school.

  14. Reconsider homework assignments which homeless students would be unable to execute or provide necessary supplies and support.

In case of major disasters resulting in large numbers of displaced students:

- Assemble a planning and response team consisting of the liaison plus other key staff, such as: a district administrator with the authority to establish and make exceptions to district policies; transportation director; school nurse; school counselors; special education staff; child nutrition staff; preschool providers; principals; adult education staff; and representatives from relief agencies.

- Coordinate with relief agencies to identify students, arrange parent meetings and on-site enrollment, and obtain information about services, housing placements, and anticipated mobility.

- Bring school administrators, special education staff, teachers, nurses, counselors, and transportation directors to sites housing large numbers of displaced students to begin orienting students and families to the school and providing appropriate services immediately. For example, after Hurricane Katrina, Individualized Education Program (IEP) meetings were conducted at the Houston Astrodome so that displaced students with special needs arrived at school with a current IEP and services were put in place immediately.

- Provide families with information about the local community, including maps, mass transit schedules, and locations of stores, services, laundromats, health clinics, government offices, and other resources for meeting basic needs.

- Legal aid services have been critical for families in disasters to procure benefits, process claims or loans, and for other reasons. Facilitate referrals to all available legal resources. For more information, contact the American Bar Association Commission on Homelessness & Poverty at (202) 662-1694 or your state or local bar association or legal services organization.

- Interrupt the enrollment process briefly to coordinate with housing placements, when appropriate, due to immediately pending moves.

- Provide mental health support for both students and parents, in school and at shelter sites.

- Conduct classroom and school-wide activities immediately and in the long-term to help students attending prior to the disaster feel secure about their place in their school and to sensitize them to the issues facing displaced students.

- See "Providing Education to Students Displaced by Natural Disasters" section at the end of this Chapter for more information.

4. Resolution of Disputes

Interruptions in education can severely damage a student's academic progress and disrupt his or her classmates and teachers. To avoid such disruptions, the McKinney-Vento Act requires immediate enrollment during disputes and provides for procedures to resolve disputes. This allows schools, parents, and youth to resolve disagreements quickly and efficiently without disrupting the classroom or the student's education.

What the Act Says:

■ *Every state must establish procedures to promptly resolve disputes regarding the educational placement of homeless students.*

■ *If a student is sent to a school other than the school of origin or the school requested by a parent/guardian or unaccompanied youth, the LEA must provide a written explanation of its decision and the right to appeal, whether or not the parent/guardian or unaccompanied youth disputes the placement.*

■ *Whenever a dispute arises, the student must be immediately admitted to the school in which enrollment is sought while the dispute is being resolved. If enrollment is in the school of origin, transportation must be provided upon request.*

■ *The school must refer the student, parent, or guardian to the local liaison to carry out the dispute resolution process as expeditiously as possible.*

■ *LEA homeless liaisons must ensure that the dispute resolution process is followed for unaccompanied youth.*

How Your School and District Can Implement the Act:

• Contact your State Coordinator for information about your state's process for resolving disputes, and develop a complementary process at the district level.

• When inter-district issues arise, make sure representatives from all involved districts are present to help resolve the dispute.

• Keep the dispute resolution process as informal and accessible as possible, consistent with impartial and complete review.

• Establish procedures for parents, guardians, and unaccompanied youth to initiate the dispute resolution process directly at the school they choose, as well as at the school district or LEA homeless liaison's office.

- Establish timelines for resolving disputes.

- Inform parents, guardians, and unaccompanied youth that they can provide written or oral documentation to support their position and that they can seek the assistance of advocates or attorneys.

- Because districts most often possess substantial resources in comparison to the families and youth with whom they work, districts should take care to implement policies and procedures which balance the conduct of disputes in a fair and respectful manner.

- Ensure privacy and confidentiality of all proceedings and information, refraining from intrusive investigations or questioning the child or youth at school or in front of neighbors or other students.

- Best practices include acknowledging that families have the sole right to make decisions affecting their lives such as when to leave a partner, when to declare bankruptcy, and what living arrangements best protect their health and safety. Schools must respect family autonomy and the right of informed consent in all these matters.

- Best practice also includes using social workers who are well trained in McKinney-Vento and experienced in working with low-income families, those with disabilities or histories of domestic violence to help assess any disputed matters. In some jurisdictions, staff funded by the SEA rather than the LEA may be best suited to play this role.

- Avoid stigmatizing the student or deterring access to school because of a dispute. When disputes result in a determination unfavorable to the student or family, appropriate steps must be taken promptly to coordinate the student's timely enrollment and attendance in the proper school.

- Provide students with all services for which they are eligible while disputes are resolved, including transportation and other services to permit full participation in school activities.

- Make written notices complete, as brief as possible, simply stated, and in a language the parent, guardian, or unaccompanied youth can understand. Written notice should include:

  1. Contact information for the LEA homeless liaison and State Coordinator, with a brief description of their roles;

Continued next page

2. A simple, detachable form that parents, guardians, or unaccompanied youth can complete and submit to the school to initiate the dispute process (the school should copy the form and return the copy to the custodial parent, guardian, or youth for their records when it is submitted);

3. A step-by-step description of how to formally dispute the school's decision;

4. Notice of the right to enroll immediately in the school of choice pending resolution of the dispute and to receive transportation to the school of origin;

5. Notice that "immediate enrollment" includes full participation in all school activities;

6. Notice of the right to obtain the assistance of advocates or attorneys;

7. Notice of the right to appeal to the state if the district-level resolution is not satisfactory; and

8. Timelines for resolving district- and state-level appeals.

Discrimination and Segregation

Most of the people who will read this booklet have never experienced homelessness but likely have encountered homeless persons on the street. Naturally, images of people living on the street affect us all. As human beings we bring our images and understandings with us when we approach our work, for good or for ill. We often fear what we do not know or understand. Such fears and limited understanding of homelessness, if not addressed, can create negative attitudes, stereotyping, and bias against homeless parents, children, and youth.

The McKinney-Vento Act affirmatively protects the civil rights of children and youth experiencing homelessness. It expressly prohibits discrimination against homeless students in the provision of educational services. It expressly prohibits the segregation of students experiencing homelessness from other students. Moreover, it challenges schools, teachers, administrators, principals, clerks, attendance officers, and student support personnel to learn about and become connected with the issue of homelessness and its impact on the learning process.

Simply stated, schools must fully integrate students experiencing homelessness into each aspect of the school's program and services. Teachers, administrators, and support personnel must be sensitive to, and aware of, the needs of homeless students while being careful not to stigmatize them or set them apart. The problems homeless families face are the same problems many other families experience, but with the added stress of extreme poverty. For most homeless families, lacking a permanent place to live is a temporary condition; a crisis through which they will pass successfully given the right support and assistance. It is neither a permanent state of being nor a permanent characteristic that defines the family or its members. Children and youth experiencing homelessness can thrive on the normalcy and safety that a stable, quality school offers. Funding provided to states under the McKinney-Vento Act may be utilized to heighten school staff awareness of homelessness and offer specific strategies which the school can utilize to effectively respond to the needs of those students. Through systemic planning and better understanding, bias can be addressed and discriminatory attitudes and practices against members of this particular population can be avoided.

What the Act Says:

- *Schools must ensure that each student experiencing homelessness has equal access to the same free, appropriate public education as provided to any other student, as well as a full and equal opportunity to succeed in those schools. Homelessness alone is not sufficient reason to separate students from the mainstream school environment.*

- *Students experiencing homelessness must be provided services comparable to those offered to other students, including: transportation, special education, gifted and talented programs, vocational services, and services for students with limited English proficiency, to name a few.*

- *LEAs (in conjunction with the SEA) must review and revise policies, rules, practices, and laws to ensure that children and youth experiencing homelessness have equal access to educational services.*

- *The LEA within a state that accepts McKinney-Vento funding (regardless of whether the LEA itself receives McKinney-Vento funding) may not create or operate schools or programs that segregate homeless students from other students,[19] nor may they provide services in settings within the school that segregate homeless students from other students.*

- *LEAs and the SEA must adopt policies and practices to ensure that students experiencing homelessness are not stigmatized or isolated.*

Schools must provide preschool-age children experiencing homelessness with equal access to the same preschool programs as other children.

Schools must provide equal access to appropriate education and support services for homeless youth, including those who have separated from school.

How Your School and District Can Implement the Act:

- Review all of the programs and services of the district and of each school to ensure that homeless families and students are meaningfully included and are fully considered in the implementation of those programs.

- Take advantage of teacher institute days and staff development time to bring in speakers, including homeless or formerly homeless parents and students to heighten awareness. Encourage staff to focus on the strengths possessed by homeless families and recognize the value of staff work when homeless students are involved, in terms of the potential for reducing student mobility, improving attendance, enhancing academic performance, and generally elevating the value of the school.

- Starting with the admissions office, create a climate in which all feel welcome and in which an attitude of sensitivity and acceptance exists.

- Be clear that discrimination against families experiencing homelessness is prohibited in every aspect of school and district services and will have an impact on staff job evaluations.

- Create opportunities for feedback from the "consumer," i.e., students and parents experiencing homelessness, to see how the school is perceived and how it might improve the perception.

Collaboration with Community Agencies

Students who are hungry, sick, traumatized, and living in highly mobile, precarious situations will face barriers to academic achievement beyond those that may exist in the school. Under the McKinney-Vento Act, schools play a critical role not just in ensuring educational stability and access, but in assisting the student and her family to access services that may address the underlying causes of homelessness as well as emergency needs.

Many homeless families (or unaccompanied minors) will have been identified as homeless by the school prior to accessing community services. Families and youth may not know what services are available or how to seek assistance. In these situations, the schools can and should connect these students and their families to appropriate services in the community. Through this approach, liaisons can help families and unaccompanied youth obtain housing stability and other services as soon as possible, thus reducing the educational disruption caused by homelessness.

In order to effectively connect students and their families with services, it is important not only for the liaison but also for the service providers to ensure that the services are accessible and appropriately tailored for the family or unaccompanied youth. Some homeless families have previous difficult experiences with social service systems due, in part, to multiple and confusing referrals. Therefore, the assistance of knowledgeable staff in directly connecting families to services for which they are clearly eligible can be a great relief.

What the Act Says:

▓ *Local liaisons must coordinate with community agencies to provide educational services; referrals to health care services, dental services, and mental health services; and other appropriate services.*

▓ *State Coordinators and LEAs must inform service providers and advocates who work with families in homeless situations of the duties of the local liaison.*

▓ *Liaisons must, as a part of their duties, coordinate and collaborate with State coordinators and community and school personnel responsible for the provision of education and related services to homeless children and youth.*

How Your School and District Can Implement the Act:

• Liaisons should schedule regular meetings with community service providers to learn about available services, create efficient and streamlined referral systems, and establish methods of sharing information.

• Liaisons should engage in local homelessness planning processes, such as the "Continuum of Care" (the local coordinating body for homeless assistance funds administered by the U.S. Department of Housing and Urban Development) or local "Ten Year Plans to End

Continued next page

Homelessness." Liaisons should ensure they are on appropriate service provider-related listervs.

- Liaisons should educate service providers about the McKinney-Vento Act and the role of school districts in supporting homeless students and provide support for service providers and the families as needed. Liaisons should also ask for assistance from service providers to increase families' involvement in school programs.

- Liaisons should think broadly about potential sources of help, including public and private agencies. Potential community collaborators include shelters, transitional housing programs, public housing agencies, motels, food banks, soup kitchens, child welfare agencies, legal aid programs, youth-serving organizations, drop-in centers, health departments, organizations facilitating health insurance enrollment under the expansion of Medicaid and the Affordable Care Act, faith-based organizations, civic organizations, parks and recreational agencies, and many more.

- Liaisons should attend and staff tables at job fairs and outreach fairs targeted toward homeless youth and families. Liaisons can educate themselves and network to educate providers about McKinney-Vento.

- Liaisons should put McKinney-Vento topics on the agenda at school and school board meetings and invite service providers to those meetings.

- Liaisons should create business cards and posters with information about the McKinney-Vento Act and ask outreach workers to distribute them to their clients.

- Liaisons should visit the NCHE Web site at *center.serve.org/ nche/ibt/sc_collab.php* for ideas about how schools, service providers and housing agencies can successfully collaborate.

Providing Education to Students
Displaced by Natural Disasters

Children and youth displaced by hurricanes and other disasters such as floods, tornadoes, and wildfires typically find themselves in temporary living situations that may include hotels, motels, trailers, shelters, cars, or sharing the housing of friends or relatives. Displaced children and youth without permanent and stable housing are considered "homeless" for education purposes. Indeed, they have much in common with young people who were made homeless for other reasons. They have similar mobility patterns and face similar educational barriers.

Providing displaced students who have yet to find permanent housing with the educational services provided under the McKinney-Vento Act promotes school stability by allowing children displaced by natural disasters to remain in their school of origin. The ability to continue in a school of origin may be limited by the best interests of the child, feasibility, or the preference of a parent or guardian. In the context of displaced students, it would not be feasible for a child living in a shelter in Florida to attend a school in New Jersey. However, transportation crossing state lines is possible for students separated by shorter distances from their school of origin if it remains in their best interest. Similarly, if the student's school of origin has been destroyed or closed as a result of a hurricane or other disaster, it would simply not be possible for the student to continue to attend school there.

Schools should inform parents that McKinney-Vento says that a school of origin can be "the school in which the child or youth was last enrolled." But, if it is not possible for students to attend their original schools, they may still be entitled to enroll in new schools close to where they are temporarily living. Once they have done so, they have established a new school of origin through the simple act of enrolling.

Schools must immediately enroll displaced students even if normally required documents are unavailable. Academic records may not be immediately available if the student was living in an area struck by a disaster, and delays may last longer than usual if schools are closed or records are destroyed.

McKinney-Vento prohibits the segregation of homeless students. Children and youth should not be confined to classrooms in shelters or other settings where they would be isolated from their non-homeless peers. The anti-segregation provisions allow children who have experienced the trauma of evacuation to quickly return to a sense of normalcy by leaving shelters each day (and other reminders of homeless status) and attending regular schools with other kids.

For more information on providing educational resources to displaced children and youth, please consult the National Law Center on Homelessness and Poverty's *Homeless Education Advocacy Manual: Disaster Advocacy Manual* published in January 2013. The Manual may be accessed at ***www.nlchp.org/content/pubs/DisasterManual%20FINAL% 204-13-133.pdf.*** The NCHE Web site also offers a series of resources to help schools respond to natural disasters at ***center.serve.org/nche/ibt/ dis_prep.php.***

CHAPTER V

Young Children Without Homes: Creating Access to Early Childhood Education Opportunities through Three Federal Laws

Homelessness has a devastating impact on the health and development of all children, including young children. Compared to non-homeless children served by Head Start, children experiencing homelessness were reported to have greater developmental delays, to be more likely to have learning disabilities and developmental delays, and to exhibit a higher frequency of socioemotional problems.[20] These statistics are especially troubling in light of the fact that over 50 percent of children living in shelters are under the age of six,[21] and therefore at an age where early childhood education can have a significant positive impact on their development and future academic achievement.[22]

This chapter reviews the policies of three federal statutes that provide access and support to young children experiencing homelessness: 1) the McKinney-Vento Act; 2) the Head Start Act; and 3) the Individuals with Disabilities Education Act. The final section combines strategies for implementing all three statutes.

The McKinney-Vento Act and Public Preschool Programs

Equal access to all school services for homeless children specifically includes equal access to preschool education. A growing understanding of the vital importance of early childhood education in the longer-term educational success of students has generated many new preschool, Head Start, and pre-kindergarten programs. In school year 2011-2012, 40 states offered preschool programs for children.[23] As preschool enrollment has risen since 2002, average state spending per child has decreased from a high of $5,020 in 2002 to a low of $3,841 per child in 2012.[24] Only 4 percent of three-year-olds and 28 percent of four-year-olds are served by state-funded preschool programs.[25] More capacity and funding are necessary to address the gap in services. Research shows that preschool programs increase academic achievement, reduce grade retention, increase lifetime earnings, promote social adjustment, reduce the incidence of crime, and decrease economic dependency on welfare. Student achievement gaps develop early in life and can be reduced or eliminated by high quality preschool.

Because a key focus of the McKinney-Vento Act is to reduce the barriers not just to enrollment or attendance but also to educational success, ensuring homeless children's access to preschool programs should be of special importance to SEAs and LEAs. Even where preschool opportunities are limited, SEAs and LEAs should make extra efforts to ensure the participation of children and families experiencing homelessness. For example, Texas state law makes homeless children automatically eligible for its limited pre-kindergarten programs and requires LEAs to notify the families of eligible children.[26]

Many preschool programs and pre-K programs are operated by schools and LEAs, but many others are operated by non-profit agencies. LEAs are responsible for ensuring access to the programs within its control and according most McKinney-Vento rights—including immediate enrollment and comparable services. For non-profit agency preschool programs not within the LEA's control and not typically subject to McKinney-Vento requirements, however, the State should exercise responsibility for ensuring the inclusion of homeless children. The source of funding for this is often state or federal monies with significant regulatory control from the SEA. States should review and revise all policies and practices, including those affecting state-funded, but privately-run, preschools to ensure equal access for homeless students.

Frequently, preschool programs in a community are a patchwork of LEA-operated, SEA-administered and private entities. Such a system can be confusing for families and act as a barrier to access.[27] Through collaboration and leadership from the LEA, families should be informed about the availability of all local preschool opportunities and assisted in gaining access. Referrals and cooperative agreements can further expand availability for homeless children and youth. For example, the homeless liaison can develop a database of available preschool programs and become an area resource for parents. The application process and the application document itself can be both simplified and standardized so that one application may act as an appropriate application for any preschool program.

What the McKinney-Vento Act Says About Preschool:

■ *State plans must include procedures that ensure each homeless preschool-age child has access to the same public preschool programs administered by the State as other children who are not homeless.*

■ *States must identify preschool-age children experiencing homelessness.*

■ *The State Coordinator must gather data on the nature and extent of problems homeless children face in gaining access to public preschool programs.*

■ *The State Coordinator must facilitate coordination between the SEA and other agencies to provide services to homeless preschoolers and collaborate with preschool program personnel.*

■ *The LEA liaison must ensure that homeless children have access to Head Start, Even Start and public preschool programs administered by the LEA.*

The Head Start Act and Homeless Children and Families

Head Start and Early Head Start are federally-funded preschool programs for low-income families. Early Head Start (EHS) serves families from the time a mother is pregnant through the time a child is age 2 years and 9 months. Head Start (HS) serves families with children from ages 2 years 9 months through 5-years-old. HS/EHS, with its family-centered approach, offers essential and invaluable supports for children and families experiencing homelessness. Mandated comprehensive services include health, dental, nutrition, educational, and family services. Despite HS/EHS focus on low-income families, homeless families face barriers to participation because of high mobility, lack of program capacity, lack of enrollment records, and lack of awareness. The reauthorization of the Head Start Act in 2007 includes many provisions intended to address these barriers and improve access to HS/EHS programs.

What the Head Start Act Says About Homeless Children:[28]

■ *The definition of homelessness in the Head Start Act is the same definition as in the education subtitle of the McKinney-Vento Homeless Assistance Act.*

■ *Homeless children are categorically eligible for Head Start.*

■ *The Secretary of the U.S. Department of Health and Human Services is required to issue regulations[29] that require Head Start agencies to:*

　　1. Ensure that homeless children are identified and prioritized for enrollment;

2. *Allow homeless families to apply to, enroll in, and attend Head Start programs while required documents are obtained within a reasonable time frame; and*

3. *Coordinate individual Head Start centers and programs with efforts to implement Subtitle VII-B of the McKinney-Vento Homeless Assistance Act.*

■ *Head Start State Collaboration Directors must develop a strategic plan that will enhance collaboration and coordination with, and services provided for homeless children.*

■ *Head Start agencies must coordinate and collaborate with programs under Subtitle VII-B of the McKinney-Vento Homeless Assistance Act.*

■ *Head Start programs must establish channels of communication between Head Start staff and McKinney-Vento liaisons to facilitate coordination of programs.*

■ *Head Start programs must develop and implement a family outreach and support program in coordination with outreach efforts under the McKinney-Vento Act.*

■ *Early Head Start programs must coordinate services with programs in the community for homeless infants and toddlers.*

IDEA: Homeless Infants, Toddlers and Preschoolers with Disabilities

IDEA outlines the services required for young children with disabilities or developmental delays. IDEA (Section 619 of Part B) requires local education agencies to provide a free, appropriate public education for children with disabilities ages three to five, based on the child's needs and in accordance with his or her Individualized Education Program (IEP). Services can follow various models, including special classrooms in a public school, services integrated into a Head Start or other preschool program, or even services provided where the child is staying. LEAs must conduct "child find" activities to ensure they identify and serve all eligible children, specifically including eligible children who are homeless. The same IDEA requirements explained in Chapter VIII regarding timelines for evaluations and implementation of IEPs apply to younger children.

Part C of IDEA provides early intervention services for infants and toddlers from birth through age two with developmental delays or conditions likely to result in a developmental delay.[30] Services are provided under state supervision by local Part C agencies and providers, including: LEAs; educational service centers; local health, developmental disabilities or mental health agencies; and private providers. Agencies must also implement procedures to identify and serve all infants and toddlers with disabilities in their service area, specifically including children experiencing homelessness ("child find").[31] Local agencies develop Individualized Family Service Plans (IFSPs), which outline the services to be provided to the child and family. The services must be offered where the child is located. This includes a shelter or home that the family is sharing with a family or relative. An important option to homeless families is having the choice to continue the IFSP when the child turns 3-years-old and IDEA Part B services begin. Under Part B, services are normally provided at the school zoned for the area where the family is residing or the preschool the child attends. Maintaining services where the child is staying may be crucial for a highly mobile family.

What IDEA Part C Says About Homeless Children and Families:

▨ *The definition of homelessness for IDEA Part C is the same definition as in the education subtitle of the McKinney-Vento Homeless Assistance Act.*

▨ *States must make early intervention services available to homeless infants and toddlers with disabilities and their families.*[32]

▨ *States must ensure the meaningful involvement of homeless families and wards of the state in the planning and implementation of the Part C program.*

▨ *States must establish a State Interagency Coordinating Council, which must include a representative of the State McKinney-Vento Coordinator and the state child welfare agency.*

How Your School and District Can Implement Federal Law to Create Access to Early Childhood Education for Young Children Experiencing Homelessness

Public Preschool Strategies

- Be familiar with the preschool procedures indicated in the McKinney-Vento state plan and implement them locally.

Continued next page

- Train LEA liaisons and all preschool staff on the definitions, rights, and needs of preschool-age children experiencing homelessness.

- Seek information from identified homeless families about the existence of preschool-age children and allow expedited enrollment without prescreening or assessment requirements. Include space on the K-12 school registration and withdrawal forms to list siblings under the age of six.

- Create an 800 number for immediate paperless registration of homeless children in preschool programs. Allow a single application to be sufficient for entry to any area preschool program.

- Publicize the existence of preschool, pre-K and Head Start programs through posters, brochures, and presentations within schools, at parent-participation events and within the community at shelters, social service organizations, public health clinics, teen parenting programs, and public aid offices.

- Provide transportation to preschool, pre-K, and Head Start programs.

- Enter into collaborative agreements with other preschool and pre-K programs not operated by the LEA which may have availability, to ensure that such programs serve homeless children.

- Develop strategies to connect with hard-to-reach families in the community to dispel reservations about enrolling children in preschool. Utilize parent-to-parent outreach and enrollment strategies.

- Public preschool programs across the country have adopted policies and procedures to provide access for preschoolers experiencing homelessness, including:

  1. Identifying an appropriate number of slots to be held open for children experiencing homelessness, and/or prioritizing them on waiting lists.

  2. Developing an online preschool locator to enable staff and parents to find suitable preschool opportunities.

  3. Including homelessness in the list of criteria for priority enrollment in preschool.

  4. Permitting flexible exceptions to preschool policies on tardiness and absences.

5. Offering flexible schedules to accommodate unstable sleep patterns and family mobility.

6. Developing a strong plan to address mobility through close coordination with families, shelters, and community agencies.

7. Providing immediate medical, developmental, and mental health screenings.

8. Emphasizing a classroom structure that limits distractions, provides a simple daily schedule, and provides strong individualized attention.

9. Including a strong family component that builds the family's capacity to support child development and education and addresses critical family needs.

Head Start Strategies

• Develop relationships with Head Start directors and family support staff and inform them of the services offered to homeless families by the school district.

• Assist Head Start programs in the identification of homeless children by referring young children of school-age siblings.

• Assist Head Start programs with their community needs assessments so that the needs of homeless families are taken into consideration in program planning and service delivery.

• Assist Head Start programs to revise their selection criteria and their point systems to ensure that homeless children are prioritized for enrollment.

• Collaborate with Head Start programs on transportation to ensure that homeless children can attend and participate regularly in Head Start programs.

• Help Head Start programs gather records, including immunization records, for young children experiencing homelessness.

• Invite Head Start staff to present at school district in-service trainings on homelessness and any local homeless task force or coalition meetings.

Continued next page

IDEA Part C Strategies

- Train school and district staff on the Part C Infants and Toddlers programs and services available in your district as well as the referral process. To find local Part C agencies, visit *ectacenter.org/contact/ptccoord.asp*.

- Train enrollment staff to ask parents if they have young children at home and if they are aware of available services for young children with special needs. Explain to parents what Part C is and how the evaluation process works, and refer parents to the Part C agency as appropriate.

- Invite Part C staff to speak about their programs and services at school staff meetings and in-service training programs.

- Have Part C staff discuss their programs and services at local family shelters, food banks, soup kitchens, and public health clinics, and leave information about programs and services at those agencies, low-cost motels, public schools, housing programs, and food banks. These strategies will help Part C programs meet their child find obligations.

- Include information about Part C and the McKinney-Vento Act in school and program newsletters, handbooks, and flyers.

- Prioritize homeless children on evaluation schedules. Work with parents, community health, and mental health providers to coordinate and expedite evaluations.

- Develop and implement interim IFSPs for highly mobile children and their families so they can receive services while evaluations are completed.

- Form a Part C advisory committee on homeless, foster, and other highly mobile children and families. The homeless education liaison, Part C agency staff, migrant education staff, parents, parent involvement specialists, special education director, child welfare staff, and other interested parties should meet regularly to develop, review, and revise policies and procedures.

CHAPTER VI

Youth

Schools face special challenges in identifying and serving adolescents who are homeless. When those youth are not in the physical custody of their parents—are "unaccompanied"—the barriers can multiply. Even in ideal circumstances adolescence is a difficult time, but it can be particularly difficult for youth experiencing homelessness. Studies have found that over half of unaccompanied youth reported physical abuse at home, while over one third reported sexual abuse.[33] Some homeless youth are rejected by their families because of their sexual orientation or gender identity (desire to express identity with, or become a member of, the opposite sex). Youth who leave abusive living arrangements are often confronted with the lack of adequate shelter or housing for unaccompanied youth as well as their legal inability as minors to consent to services or enter lease agreements. Many family shelters will not accept older male youth, thus forcing them to be separated from their families. Youth living on the street are in significant danger as they are targets for adult sexual exploitation and assault. These dangers, coupled with the lack of adequate health care, place unaccompanied homeless adolescents in serious jeopardy.

Whether a youth is a runaway, "throwaway"/"pushout" (locked out or abandoned by parents), living with parents in a shelter, doubled-up, or separated from the family by economic circumstance, schools are obligated to find ways, as the McKinney-Vento Act states, to "attract, engage, and retain" these youth in school. One major difficulty for older youth can be problems meeting the credit requirements for advancement and graduation in high school. Missing certain courses or even a portion of a semester may result in loss of credit which in turn may preclude advancing to the next grade or graduating on time. Some youth have separated from school because they fell too far behind or did not feel safe or cared about in school. Reaching and serving these youth presents great opportunities to protect them from violence and set them on a path to success in adulthood.

What the Act Says:

■ *Unaccompanied youth are entitled to the same rights as other homeless students and must be provided with information about those rights, including school transportation and other services.*

■ Schools must serve homeless youth whether or not the youth is in the physical custody of a parent or guardian.

■ Local liaisons have special duties to assist unaccompanied youth in determining school choice, enrolling the student, and obtaining transportation. Liaisons must help unaccompanied youth choose and enroll in a school, after considering the youth's wishes, and provide youth with notice of their right to appeal decisions counter to their wishes. School districts must provide transportation to and from the school of origin for unaccompanied youth at the liaison's request.

■ If an appeal is necessary, local liaisons must facilitate this process for unaccompanied youth.

■ Schools must learn about and address the barriers encountered by homeless youth in enrolling, attending, and succeeding in school, including guardianship considerations and other issues.

■ Special attention shall be given by schools to ensure the enrollment and attendance of homeless youth who are not currently attending school. Liaisons and schools must provide activities and services that enable homeless youth to enroll in, attend, and succeed in school.

■ Homeless youth and youth separated from school must be identified and accorded equal access to secondary education and support services.

How Your School and District Can Implement the Act:

- Train all staff on the special concerns and issues of homeless and unaccompanied youth. Personal and consistent attention by staff skilled at working with adolescents is a must. Make special efforts to train enrollment staff on the McKinney-Vento enrollment requirements and procedures for enrolling unaccompanied youth.

- Create a welcoming and supportive environment for homeless youth in which immediate needs for clothing, food, and hygiene can be met without stigmatizing the youth.

- Develop course, credit, and schedule flexibility so that lost school time can be recovered promptly and the youth can maintain employment while advancing through school. Access to summer school programs should be ensured.

- Review and revise policies and practices that impose limitations on the right of older youth to re-enter high school.

- Review and revise policies and practices that may limit the right of homeless youth to join clubs or participate on athletic teams.

- Utilize truancy or attendance officers to connect with youth in the community by offering needed assistance in a nonjudgmental way.

- Build relationships with youth service agencies, youth officers, and juvenile court staff to help in identifying and referring youth to school.

- Conduct outreach at youth shelters, libraries, drop-in centers, and street locations where homeless youth gather.

- Revise or develop LEA policies to address issues related to who authorizes unaccompanied youth to participate in field trips or extracurricular activities. Work with legal staff to eliminate any fears about potential liability.

- Maintain a listing of available surrogate parents to assist unaccompanied youth with their special education needs (see Chapter VII).

- If your state has runaway reporting requirements designed to reconnect youth with their parents, help the youth avoid the trauma of arrest by developing youth-centered approaches of achieving family reunification. For instance, when appropriate and safe, try to get youth to call home or consent to school personnel calling their parents and letting them know where they are. Refer youth to federally-financed youth shelters or other programs that focus on reconnecting runaways and families. Develop partnerships with your local social services agency and refer youth to that agency first rather than to law enforcement.

- Develop relationships with local legal aid attorneys so that youth can obtain advice and representation on issues including access to services, a safe place to live, and public benefits.

- Help unaccompanied youth go to college by assisting them to obtain independent student status on their financial aid applications (FAFSA).

CHAPTER VII

Students Involved in the Child Welfare System (Foster Care)

Similar to children experiencing homelessness, children in out-of-home care due to abuse and neglect often struggle academically. Studies demonstrate that the nearly 400,000 students in foster care experience: high rates of school mobility when they enter care and when they change living placements, delays in enrollment when school changes occur, school suspensions and expulsions at higher rates than their peers not in foster care, lower standardized test scores in reading and math, high levels of grade retention and drop-out, and far lower high school and college graduation rates.[34]

Foster children often experience high rates of mobility. Some of this mobility is due to the temporary nature of foster care. Fifteen percent of children in foster care stay in care for one month or less, and another 16 percent remain in care for five months or less.[35] Over half of all children who leave foster care will return home to their parents.[36] However, many children in foster care remain in care for a longer time, despite efforts to secure a more permanent home.[37]

Students in foster care have an average of 2.8 living placements during their time in care, including the initial move when they enter care.[38] This mobility in living situations often leads to mobility in school placements. One regional study of students revealed substantial levels of school mobility associated with placement in out-of-home care.[39] Over one-third of young adults reported having had five or more school changes.[40]

What the Act Says:

- *The definition of children eligible under the McKinney-Vento Act includes "children awaiting foster care placement." While this term has not been defined in federal law or regulations, many states and jurisdictions have created their own definition. There is a wide variety of definitions, and it is important to know how your jurisdiction defines this term. To access a full list of state interpretations of "awaiting foster care placement," please see the State Chart compiled by the Legal Center for Foster Care and Education.[41]*

- *The definition of students eligible under the McKinney-Vento Act includes children or youth who lack a "fixed, regular, and adequate nighttime resi-*

dence." Because foster care by definition is temporary, many children and youth in care have placements that may not be fixed or regular. Some states and jurisdictions have used this rationale to determine which students in foster care are eligible under McKinney-Vento. Still, while many states and jurisdictions have included some children in foster care as eligible for the protections of the McKinney-Vento Act, schools and child welfare agencies must nonetheless work together to ensure that all children in foster care are provided the school stability and continuity they so desperately need and deserve. A variety of states have passed laws or policy to support school stability for children in foster care, including granting them the right to remain in the same school regardless of residency, including transportation, and the right to immediate enrollment in a new school when in their best interest. Also, recognizing how important McKinney-Vento liaisons have been, some states have created similar positions for children in foster care. To access a chart detailing state laws and policies supporting school stability for children in foster care, please visit: **www.fostercareandeducation.org/ Database. aspx?EntryId=1861&Command=Core_Download&method=inline**

How Your School and District Can Implement the Act:

- Train all staff on the special concerns and issues of children in foster care and living in out-of-home placements.

- Create a trauma sensitive environment for children who have experienced abuse and neglect in their home lives.

- Build relationships with child welfare system professionals, including local child welfare agencies and workers, child advocates, and local foster parents.

Fostering Connections to Success and Increasing Adoptions Act

In October 2008, the Fostering Connections to Success and Increasing Adoptions Act of 2008 (P.L. 110-351, Fostering Connections Act) was signed into law. Among its provisions to address the needs of children and youth in foster care, it includes important new requirements for child welfare agencies and local education agencies to promote education stability for children in care. Similar to McKinney-Vento, the Fostering Connections Act requires child welfare agencies to document in their case plans coordination with local education agencies to ensure children remain in their original school when there is a change in living placement.

If it is not in the child's best interest to remain in the original school, child welfare agency and local education agencies must ensure that the child is immediately enrolled in a new school, with all necessary records.

Frequently Asked Questions:

Q: Who is eligible under each law and can some children be eligible under both?

A: Children eligible under the McKinney-Vento Act and the Fostering Connections Act may overlap. For example, if a child is in out-of-home care and also meets the definition of awaiting foster care placement, both Fostering Connections and McKinney-Vento apply. State laws may also apply. The application of one law does not diminish the rights provided by the others. Rather, each law adds a layer of rights and protections for children, based on their circumstances and needs.

Q: How should child welfare and education agencies navigate the two laws?

A: Fostering Connections, McKinney-Vento, and other federal and state education and child welfare laws must work together to support students in foster care. To ensure proper implementation of federal and state laws for children in out-of-home care, child welfare supervisors, caseworkers, and other advocates should meet with school district McKinney-Vento liaisons, special education directors, and other administrators. Meetings should address topics such as best interest determinations, transportation plans, enrollment protocols, and record transfers. Communication and collaboration among education and child welfare professionals are critical to support school success for children in out-of-home care.

Q: Does Fostering Connections impact eligibility for McKinney-Vento protections for children in out-of-home care?

A: No. The passage of Fostering Connections, a child welfare law, does not change the rights and protections of McKinney-Vento. Children in out-of-home care may continue to be eligible under McKinney-Vento if they are living in transitional or emergency shelters, are "awaiting foster care placement," or are unaccompanied homeless youth.

Q: How should best interest school selection decisions be made under Fostering Connections and McKinney-Vento and who should make these determinations?

A: The passage of Fostering Connections, a child welfare law, does not change in any way the best interest determination for children who qualify for McKinney-Vento. This decision is still made by the McKinney-Vento liaison. Just as before, best practice suggests that the McKinney-Vento liaison should gather information about a child from the child, foster parent, child's caseworker, and child advocate or attorney in making a best interest determination. While the input of a caseworker is very critical in making a best interest determination under the McKinney-Vento Act, it is only the McKinney-Vento liaison and parent who will ultimately make this decision. However, when a child in out-of-home care is not eligible for McKinney-Vento, the rights of Fostering Connections still apply. As such, it may be the child welfare agencies' responsibility to make the best interest determinations. Best practice would suggest that education agency staff should be consulted in making these decisions.

Q: What is the role of the parent in making education decisions?

A: Unless a court has limited a parent's education rights, the parent continues to be the decisionmaker for all special and general education decisions. This is true under both Fostering Connections and McKinney-Vento.

Q: How is transportation covered under both laws?

A: Children in care who are eligible under McKinney-Vento and require transportation to remain in their schools of origin are still entitled to transportation under McKinney-Vento by the education agency. However, child welfare agencies should collaborate to support these efforts as much as possible. For children in care not eligible under McKinney-Vento, child welfare agencies may use federal ("IV-E") foster care maintenance or administrative dollars to support transportation to keep children in the same school. While this is an allowable reimbursement, it is not mandatory. However, since the agency is required to ensure that when in a child's best interest he or she remains in the same school, providing transportation will often be necessary to comply with this requirement.

How Your School and District Can Implement Fostering Connections:

- Educate your school and district staff about Fostering Connections; determine if a staff person needs to be identified to oversee the implementation of the Act.

- Share knowledge and experience working with McKinney-eligible children to help inform school policies and procedures related to Fostering Connections.

- Work to create policies on how to determine which Act applies, and procedures for when the two laws overlap and students are eligible under both.

- Coordinate with local placement agencies to ensure that parents, foster parents, surrogate parents, youth, other caregivers, and caseworkers are aware of these rights and how to invoke them.

Other Important Laws Related to Foster Care
Healthy, Hunger-Free Kids Act (Public Law 111-296)

The Act, enacted in 2010, amends a key provision of the National School Lunch Act (42 USC 1758) to make any foster child categorically eligible, without the necessity of an application, for free school meals if their "care and placement is the responsibility (of an agency that administers a state IV-B or IV-E plan)" or if a "court has placed (the child) with a caretaker household". To verify eligibility, a local educational agency just needs documentation from an appropriate state or local child welfare agency indicating that a child is a foster child under state responsibility or has been placed in a caretaker household by a court.

College Cost Reduction Act

The complexities of the financial aid process often create a barrier for youth in foster care to apply to and enroll in higher education. The College Cost Reduction Act makes clear that for the purposes of federal financial aid, an "independent student" includes a youth who is "an orphan, in foster care, or a ward of the court at any time when the individual was 13 years of age or older." This provision significantly increases the number of former and current youth in care who may fall into this category. If a youth is considered "independent," only the youth's income, not that of a parent or guardian, is considered in determining eligibility for financial aid. (See also Chapter X)

Higher Education Opportunity Act

In August 2008, the Higher Education Opportunity Act was enacted. This legislation reauthorizes the Higher Education Act and includes numerous amendments designed to increase homeless and foster students' access to postsecondary education.

The Federal TRIO programs consist of programs that support at-risk junior high and high school students to graduate from high school, enter college, and complete their degrees. These programs include Talent Search, Upward Bound, Student Support Services, Educational Opportunity Centers, Staff Development Activities, and Gaining Early Awareness and Readiness for Undergraduate Programs (GEAR-UP). Students experiencing homelessness or in foster care are at great risk of academic failure due to their extreme poverty and residential instability, yet, prior to this reauthorization, they were not specifically mentioned or targeted by any of the TRIO programs.

The law now requires that "the Secretary shall, as appropriate, require each applicant for funds under the [TRIO] program... to identify and make available services under such program, including mentoring, tutoring, and other services provided by such program, to foster care youth (including youth in care and youth who have left care after reaching age 13)...". Furthermore, the law makes homeless children and youth, or youth in foster care (including youth who have left foster care after reaching age 13), automatically eligible for all TRIO programs.

In addition, the law makes clear that services and programs such as counseling, mentoring, tutoring, can be "specially designed for" "homeless students, those in or aging out of foster care and disconnected youth."

Finally, and importantly, the law also makes clear that Student Support Services funds can be used for "securing temporary housing during breaks in the academic year for students who are (A) homeless or formerly homeless under McKinney or (B) in foster care or aging out of the foster care system." (See also Chapter X)

CHAPTER VIII

Students with Disabilities in Homeless Situations: Requirements of Part B of the Individuals with Disabilities Education Act[42]

The physical conditions and emotional repercussions of homelessness take a toll on students. Studies indicate that children who are homeless are twice as likely to have learning disabilities and three times as likely to have an emotional disturbance as children who are not homeless.[43] These disabilities can significantly affect a student's capacity to succeed in school.

The federal law known as the Individuals with Disabilities Education Act (IDEA) protects the rights of children and youth with disabilities.[44] IDEA is designed to ensure that all students with disabilities receive a free, appropriate public education, including special education and related services. Special education is defined as specially designed instruction provided at no cost to the parents to meet the unique needs of a child with a disability. Related services include transportation, physical therapy, psychological services, social work services, and counseling, among others. Congress reauthorized IDEA in 2004, and the U.S. Department of Education updated its agency regulations in 2006.[45]

To be eligible for IDEA services, students must require special education to benefit from school, due to a disability. Parents can request that the school conduct evaluations to determine eligibility. The school must conduct all necessary evaluations within timelines established by the state, or within 60 days of the parent's request if the state has not established timelines. If the student is eligible for IDEA services, the school must design an Individualized Education Program or Plan (IEP), which determines the student's services and educational goals. Part C of IDEA provides services for infants and toddlers with disabilities from birth through age two, according to the child's Individualized Family Service Plan (IFSP).

Despite IDEA's protections, students who are homeless and have disabilities often do not receive the special education services for which they are eligible. Barriers to services include:

- Difficulty recognizing potential disabilities due to the mobility and emotional stress caused by homelessness;
- Lack of an available parent or surrogate to request evaluations and represent the child or unaccompanied youth;
- Difficulty completing evaluations and determining eligibility due to the student's mobility and school transfers;
- Inconsistent implementation of the IEP due to the student's mobility and school transfers; and
- Lack of timely transfer of records when enrolling in a new school.

IDEA's 2004 amendments and 2006 regulations address these barriers. They also contain provisions to assist states and school districts in implementing both IDEA and the McKinney-Vento Act in a coordinated manner. Together, IDEA and the McKinney-Vento Act ensure that students with disabilities in homeless situations receive the services they need.

What IDEA Says:

▨ *The definition of "homeless children" in the IDEA is the same as in the McKinney-Vento Act.*

▨ *States must ensure that homeless children with disabilities are identified, located, and evaluated.*

▨ *"Parent" includes biological, adoptive or foster parents, guardians, individuals legally responsible for the child's welfare, or individuals acting in the place of a parent and with whom the child lives. The latter category specifically includes grandparents, stepparents, or other relatives, but the individual does not necessarily have to be a relative.*[46]

▨ *LEAs must appoint surrogate parents for unaccompanied homeless youth, recognizing that such youth often do not have an adult in their lives who meets the definition of "parent." LEAs must make reasonable efforts to complete the appointment process within 30 days of determining that a surrogate is needed.*

▨ *LEAs must develop procedures to appoint temporary surrogate parents for unaccompanied homeless youth while appointment of a surrogate parent is pending. Temporary surrogates can be appropriate staff members of emergency shelters, transitional shelters, independent living programs, street outreach programs, the state, the LEA, or another agency involved in the education or care of the youth, as long as the staff member has adequate knowledge and skills and does not have a personal or professional interest that conflicts with the interest of the youth.*

▓ *Each public agency must ensure that the rights of unaccompanied homeless youth are protected.*

▓ *LEAs are no longer required to obtain parental consent for initial evaluations of foster children[47] if the LEA cannot find the parent, the parent's rights have been terminated, or a judge has removed the parent's educational decision-making rights and appointed another person to represent the child.*

▓ *Judges may appoint surrogate parents for foster children.*

▓ *LEAs must ensure that evaluations of students who change LEAs during the school year are coordinated with prior schools as expeditiously as possible to ensure prompt completion of full evaluations.*

▓ *LEAs must complete evaluations for students who change LEAs within regular timelines. The only exception to the timelines is if the LEA is making sufficient progress to ensure a prompt completion of the evaluation and the parent and LEA agree to a specific time when the evaluation will be completed.*

▓ *LEAs must immediately provide a free appropriate education for students with current IEPs who change LEAs during the school year. This specifically requires providing services comparable to those described in the previous IEP, in consultation with the parents. The LEA can then either adopt the previous IEP or implement a new IEP. If the LEA is in a new state, the LEA can conduct new evaluations if determined necessary.*

▓ *Enrolling schools must promptly obtain transfer students' records from the previous school, and previous schools must promptly respond to records requests.*

▓ *States must ensure that the requirements of the McKinney-Vento Act are met for all homeless students with disabilities in the state.*

▓ *Every state must have an IDEA State Advisory Panel, which must include state and local McKinney-Vento personnel, as well as a representative of the state child welfare agency.*

How Your School and District Can Implement IDEA for Students in Homeless Situations:

• Train special education staff as well as liaisons on the McKinney-Vento Act and the IDEA requirements related to homeless students.

• Train enrollment staff on the McKinney-Vento Act's immediate

Continued next page

enrollment and school of origin provisions and how to identify homeless students, including those with disabilities.

- Develop clear state and district policies to implement the IDEA's provisions on homeless students, and train special education staff and liaisons on those policies.

- Develop a simple, expedited procedure for appointing temporary surrogates for unaccompanied youth. The procedure should include talking with the youth about the process, asking the youth to suggest someone appropriate to serve as a temporary surrogate, and talking with that candidate to ensure that he/she has a basic understanding of the process and does not have interests that conflict with those of the youth.

- Expedite standard surrogate parent appointment procedures for unaccompanied youth.

- Train enrollment staff to ask parents and unaccompanied youth who transfer into the district about past referrals for special education evaluations and special education services, avoiding jargon and technical terms.

- Immediately request records for students in homeless situations, and maintain records for these students so that you can quickly respond to requests for records from subsequent schools. While waiting for records, contact the special education team, school counselor, and/or teachers at the previous school to ask about the student's educational placement and needs.

- Assist parents in homeless situations and unaccompanied youth to request special education evaluations if needed.

- Expedite evaluations for homeless students. Move their evaluations up on waiting lists, recognizing that their mobility places them at risk of long delays in evaluations.

- Implement appropriate supportive services immediately, while evaluations are in progress. Services such as academic support, behavior management interventions, priority seating, and mentors can be extremely helpful, yet need not be labeled as "special education."

- Consult with the special education team to see if interim IEPs or other interim special education or related services can be provided while evaluations are in progress.

- Inform parents in homeless situations and unaccompanied youth of their rights under IDEA and the McKinney-Vento Act.

- Implement existing IEPs immediately when students transfer into the district. Expedite IEP meetings to adopt the previous IEP or develop a new one.

- Be flexible regarding the time and location of IEP meetings, recognizing that parents in homeless situations may have difficulty arranging transportation and may be juggling many appointments and responsibilities in their efforts to secure housing.

- Organize regular meetings between district special education staff and the McKinney-Vento liaison to ensure a mutual understanding of roles and responsibilities and strong collaborations to meet the needs of homeless students with disabilities.

- Develop clear policies to help district staff navigate the intersections of IDEA and the McKinney-Vento Act, paying particular attention to transportation, school of origin, and immediate enrollment.

- At the state level, develop protocols to determine financial responsibility for transportation and tuition payments for homeless students with disabilities who are attending out-of-district placements due to their special needs or their homelessness.

- In anticipation of inter-district mobility, organize regular meetings among special education staff and liaisons from area school districts. Get to know one another's policies and procedures, and collaboratively develop policies and procedures to expedite evaluations for highly mobile students.

- Include parents in homeless situations and unaccompanied youth in district and school planning activities around IDEA implementation.

CHAPTER IX

Supporting Academic Achievement: Title I, Part A Requirements on Homelessness

The purpose of Title I of the Elementary and Secondary Education Act (ESEA) is to "ensure that all children have a fair, equal, and significant opportunity to obtain a high-quality education and reach, at a minimum, proficiency on challenging state academic achievement standards and state academic assessments."[48] Title I includes several provisions to ensure that homeless students benefit from its programs and services. In addition, federal regulations on Title I require that homeless students be included in assessment and accountability systems.

What the Title I, Part A Statute Says:

▓ *A student who is homeless and is attending any school in the district is eligible for Title I, Part A services.*

▓ *Before otherwise allocating funds, LEAs must reserve (or set aside) funds as are necessary to provide homeless students who do not attend Title I, Part A participating schools with services comparable to those provided to students in participating schools, including providing educationally related support services to students in shelters and other locations where students may live.*

▓ *The LEA may receive funding under Title I, Part A only if the LEA has a plan that is coordinated with the McKinney-Vento Homeless Assistance Act. The plan must be approved by and on file with the SEA.*

▓ *Each LEA Title I, Part A plan must include a description of the services that will be provided to homeless students, including services provided with funds from the Reservation of Funds set-aside.*

▓ *Any state desiring to receive funding under Title I, Part A must submit to the Secretary of the U.S. Department of Education a plan that is coordinated with the McKinney-Vento Homeless Assistance Act.*

What the Title I, Part A Regulations Say:

▓ *States must include homeless students in their academic assessment, reporting, and accountability systems, consistent with the local accountability provisions of the statute.*

What the U.S. Department of Education Guidance Says:

▦ *School districts may use reserved Title I funds to provide homeless students with services that are not ordinarily provided to other Title I students and that are not available from other sources (e.g., using reserved funds to provide clothing to meet a school's dress or uniform requirements).*

▦ *In addition to serving homeless students not enrolled in Title I schools, set-asides may also be used to provide services to homeless students who are attending Title I schools.*

How Your School and District Can Implement the Act:

• Ensure collaboration between local Title I coordinators and LEA homeless liaisons using a local plan that identifies ways that Title I will serve children and youth experiencing homelessness.

• Ensure that the needs of students experiencing homelessness are taken into account in the needs assessments that are required for school-wide programs. Establish a formula or other method to ensure that sufficient Title I funds are set aside for homeless students. For more information on calculating the mandatory set aside, visit **center.serve.org/nche/downloads/calculating_setasides.pdf.**

• Make appropriate testing accommodations for homeless students. For example, provide opportunities to make up tests if children are absent on testing day.

• Ensure that local liaisons are trained to collect achievement data for all homeless students and that district records systems enable this data collection while taking into account confidentiality issues. Use Title I funds to meet basic needs of students experiencing homelessness (e.g., clothing, supplies, health) so they may participate fully in school. In determining appropriate expenditures for the funds set aside for homeless students, it is important to note that comparable services do not mean services that are necessarily identical to other Title I, Part A services (see U.S. Department of Education Guidance).

- Use Title I funds for parent involvement, making special efforts to reach out to parents of homeless students.

- Use set aside funds for outreach services to students living in motels, shelters, transitional living programs, and other temporary residences.

- Pool Title I and McKinney-Vento funds to provide a comprehensive program for students at risk of failure, ensuring that the specific needs of students who are experiencing homelessness or high mobility, and the mandates of the McKinney-Vento Act, are met.

- Involve homeless education program staff in school improvement dialogue and projects; make sure that addressing the needs of highly mobile students is included in the school improvement plans—not addressed as a separate issue.

- Ensure LEA homeless liaison representation on the State's Committee of Practitioners, which advises the sate on carrying out its Title I responsibilities.

CHAPTER X

From Homelessness to Higher Education: Financial Aid and College Access

Many students who experience homelessness wish to pursue a college education, yet face challenges in accessing financial aid and college access programs. Inadequate college readiness, the complexity of the financial aid process, and lack of housing and support services create barriers to post-secondary education. Fortunately, recent amendments to the Higher Education Act address these challenges and provide more support for homeless students. It is important for educators and service providers to be aware of these provisions because college can be a powerful motivation for students to complete high school, as well as the best opportunity for them to escape poverty and realize their dreams.

Financial Aid

Due to their severe poverty, homeless youth are extremely unlikely to be able to access postsecondary education without federal student aid. The Free Application for Federal Student Aid (FAFSA) is the federal application form that students must complete in order to apply for virtually all types of financial aid: Pell Grants, State Grants, Institutional Grants, Tuition Waivers, Work Study, and Loans. The FAFSA requires all students not considered "independent" to provide financial information from their parents or guardians in order to determine student eligibility for aid; the application also requires a parental/guardian signature. While these requirements are logical for most applicants, they can create an insurmountable barrier for unaccompanied homeless youth, who do not receive financial support from their parents and do not have access to parental information.

What the Higher Education Act Says:

> ▨ *The definition of "independent student" for the Free Application for Federal Student Aid (FAFSA) now includes youth who have been verified during the school year in which the application is submitted as either an*

unaccompanied homeless youth, or an unaccompanied youth who is at risk of homelessness and is also self-supporting. These youth can apply for federal aid without parental information or signature.

■ *Verification of unaccompanied homeless youth status must be made by one of the following: (1) a McKinney-Vento Act school district liaison;[49] (2) a U.S. Department of Housing and Urban Development homeless assistance program director or their designee; (3) a Runaway and Homeless Youth Act program director or their designee; or (4) a financial aid administrator.*

College Access and Support Programs

The Federal TRIO programs consist of programs that support at-risk junior high and high school students to graduate from high school, enter college, and complete their degrees. These programs include Talent Search, Upward Bound, Student Support Services, Educational Opportunity Centers, Staff Development Activities, and Gaining Early Awareness and Readiness for Undergraduate Programs (GEAR UP). Students experiencing homelessness are at great risk of academic failure due to their extreme poverty and residential instability, yet, prior to this recent reauthorization, they were not specifically mentioned or targeted by the TRIO or GEAR UP programs.

What the Higher Education Act Says:

■ *Applicants for TRIO programs must identify and make available services, including mentoring, tutoring, and other services, to homeless children and youth.*

■ *Homeless children and youth are automatically eligible for TRIO programs.*

■ *Federal TRIO programs and GEAR UP program activities may include specially designed services for homeless children and youth.*

■ *The Student Support Services Program may provide assistance in securing temporary housing during breaks in the academic year for homeless students.*

■ *Staff Development Activities must include training on strategies for recruiting and serving homeless children and youth.*

■ *GEAR UP entities that are not using a cohort approach must include homeless children and youth as priority students.*

How Your School and District Can
Support Implementation of the Higher Education Act:

- Ensure that high school counselors are aware of the definition of unaccompanied youth as well as the changes to the FAFSA that enable these youth to access financial aid.

- Ensure that all Runaway and Homeless Youth Act providers, and all HUD Homeless Assistance providers, know that they are authorized to verify a youth's status as homeless and unaccompanied for financial aid purposes.

- Develop relationships with local financial aid administrators to inform them about unaccompanied homeless youth, the role of school district liaisons in identifying and assisting these young people, and the new FAFSA provisions. These provisions are very new, and many financial aid administrators have not had experience with the McKinney-Vento Act's definition of homelessness or school district liaisons.

- Use a form to facilitate communication and verification of unaccompanied homeless youth status between schools, service providers, and colleges. A template which may be modified and should be put on agency letterhead is available at *www.naehcy.org/educational-resources/higher-ed.*

- Ensure that all educators and service providers who work with unaccompanied homeless youth inform unaccompanied homeless youth that they can go to college, even without parental financial support. Too often, unaccompanied youth assume that college is not an option for them because they are unaware of processes to access financial aid.

- Support unaccompanied homeless youth throughout the financial aid process, including by connecting them to college access organizations and events such as College Goal Sunday *(www.collegegoalsundayusa.org).* Navigating the financial aid system can be difficult for students with parents; young people who are homeless and trying to survive on their own will need caring adults to help guide them and encourage their persistence.

- Help youth go to college, and stay in college, by assisting them to find scholarships for which they are eligible. Student Aid on the

Continued next page

Web at *www.studentaid.ed.gov* and *www.FinAid.org* are two excellent places to begin a search for scholarships.

• Locate and develop a relationship with a state or local college access organization in your community. College access organizations provide counseling, advice, and financial assistance. A directory is available at *www.coenet.us*.

• See if your community is served by a TRIO or GEAR UP program by accessing an online national directory at the Council for Opportunity in Education at www.coenet.us. If a TRIO or GEAR UP program is in your area, establish a relationship with appropriate staff to let them know of the needs of the homeless students in your school district and to discuss ways to collaborate.

• Establish a local or state task force on higher education and homeless students to identify barriers and develop collaborative relationships including counselors, school district liaisons, homeless service providers, financial aid administrators, admissions officers, and other college support personnel.

• Establish a point of contact for homeless students at each institute of higher education to serve as a bridge between service agencies and to assist both students and educators in addressing barriers that may arise.

NAEHCY Higher Education Helpline

For assistance with issues related to students experiencing homelessness accessing higher education, contact the NAEHCY Higher Education Helpline at 1-855-446-2673 (toll free) or *highered@naehcy.org.*

The NAEHCY Higher Education Helpline offers assistance to:

Financial Aid Administrators seeking to assist students experiencing homelessness with accessing financial aid.

Higher Education Professionals seeking to link homeless students with the supports they need to succeed in college.

High School Counselors seeking to assist homeless students with applying to and finding resources to pay for college.

State Coordinators for Homeless Education and Local Homeless Education Liaisons seeking to understand what educational rights students experiencing homelessness have in regards to college access and what support options may be available to them.

Shelter Staff and Service Providers seeking to connect youth they are serving with resources to access higher education.

Unaccompanied Homeless Youth who want to attend college but aren't sure what options are available to them to assist in paying for it.

Parents of students experiencing homelessness who wish to understand what supports may be available to their children to help them attend college.

CHAPTER XI

Relevant Federal Guidance

Highlights of recent relevant federal guidance from the U.S. Department of Education and the Agency for Children and Families are highlighted below.

Provision of Services for Homeless Students with Disabilities

Dear Colleague Letter, U.S. Department of Education, Office of Special Education and Rehabilitative Services (July 19, 2013)

The Letter provides that:

- *highly mobile children should have timely and expedited evaluations and eligibility determinations, and such determinations must not be delayed by a Response to Intervention (RTI) process; and*

- *comparable services include services during the summer, such as Extended School Year (ESY) services.*

Dear Colleague Letter, U.S. Department of Education, Office of Special Education and Rehabilitative Services (August 5, 2013)

The Letter provides that:

- *both McKinney-Vento Act and IDEA Part B funds may be used to transport homeless children with disabilities to their school of origin;*

- *the use of IDEA Part B funds to transport non-disabled homeless children in vehicles purchased for disabled students may be permissible; and*

- *where a disabled homeless students moves to a shelter in a new school district but attends the school of origin at the previous school district, under the IDEA, both school districts have a responsibility to coordinate in order to ensure the student receives a free and appropriate education.*

Provision of Early Child Care and Education for Homeless Students

Dear Colleague Letter, Department of Health & Human Services, Administration for Children and Families (January 2013)

The Letter provides the following recommendations:

- *homeless families should be given priority status in accessing Head Start and Child Care and Development Fund (CCDF) programs;*

- *policies and procedures should ensure that families who are displaced by disasters have streamlined access to services;*

- *provide increased flexibility (such as grace periods) for homeless families to submit required documentation;*

- *coordinate with homeless education state coordinators and local liaisons to assist homeless children and families in accessing resources; and*

- *participate in community homeless coalitions to ensure that services are made available to homeless families.*

For more information on creating policies and procedures to increase access to early care and education services for homeless children and families, see guidance from the Department of Health and Human Services available online at, *http://www.acf.hhs.gov/programs/occ/resource/policies-resources-for-expanding-ece-services-for-homeless-children.*

CHAPTER XII

Case Summaries

Highlights of pertinent litigation related to the McKinney-Vento Act and the educational rights of children and youth experiencing homelessness are included below.

Right to Attend School during Pendency of Appeal

N.J. v. State of New York (E.D.N.Y. Dec. 13, 2011),
No. 11-CV-5935 (ADS)(AKT)

In December 2011, N.J., whose home was destroyed by fire, filed suit against the Malverne Union Free School District and the New York State Department of Education, alleging that they denied children the rights afforded to homeless children in obtaining free public education under the Act and New York Education Law. N.J. sought to prevent the defendants from disenrolling the children from the schools they currently attended.

The court found that: (1) the mother was likely to succeed on merits of her claim that defendants violated the Act by denying the children to remain enrolled in school while the appeal was pending; (2) it was likely that irreparable harm would result if the children had to change schools twice in a relatively short time period if the appeal was successful; and (3) the balance of equities and public interests weighed in favor of the children receiving an uninterrupted education. Accordingly, the court granted the preliminary injunction, which allowed the children to continue attending their school of origin.

This case is important because it established that a denial of a stay of disenrollment pending appeal violates the McKinney Vento Act, which requires that the child "shall immediately be admitted to the school in which enrollment is sought, pending resolution of the dispute."

Rights of Foster Care Youth

Div. of Family Servs. v. N S C P (Del. Fam. Ct. Aug. 16, 2011),
No. CS11-01668 (Unpublished Opinion)

This case involved J, a 17-year-old special education student in the custody of the Division of Family Services (Division) of Delaware. In 2011, J was sent to a respite bed (care services for those with disabilities, chronic or terminal illnesses, or the elderly) located in a different school district from her school of origin. The Division advised the court that J would begin the new school year in the new school district, instead of the school of origin she was attending at the time she entered respite, to which the school district would not transport her due to limited funds.

The court framed the issue as one involving a foster child's public education rights, stating that Delaware had adopted a more comprehensive definition of child homelessness than the Act and, as such, each child in state care was entitled to protections under the Act. Accordingly, the court held that if the child or parent desired for the child to continue to attend the school of origin, then the child should continue to attend the school of origin, if feasible, and the local education agency of the school of origin must assume the responsibility of determining if it was in the best interest of the child, to the extent feasible, to do so. Because J's stated desire to return to her school of origin was not considered in this case, the court ruled that the mandates of the Act were not followed and the Division did not meet its statutory duty of assuring that it coordinated with the appropriate local educational agency to ensure the best interests of the child concerned.

Removing Barriers to Education

Kaleuati v. Tonda, Civil Action No. 07-504 (D. Haw. Oct. 6, 2007)

Lawyers for Equal Justice, the ACLU of Hawaii and Alston Hunt Floyd & Ing represented three homeless families who alleged that they had been denied access to education and, on behalf of all homeless families statewide, filed a class action lawsuit against Hawaii seeking statewide injunctive relief to remove policies that violated the Act, and to ensure that homeless children would have full, meaningful access to a public education. On August 12, 2008, the court approved a final settlement, which required the Hawaii Department of Education and Board of Education to: (1) run additional school buses (or provide reimbursement for alternative methods of transportation) and/or modify existing school bus routes to pick up homeless children; (2) hire additional homeless liaisons to assist homeless families in navigating the public school system; (3) inform homeless students and families of their rights under the Act; (4) conduct yearly trainings of school personnel; (5) modify its enrollment forms and computer systems to facilitate the enrollment process and improve attendance for homeless children; and (6) take affirmative steps to avoid stigmatizing homeless families.

NLCHP v. New York State, Civil Action No. 04 0705
(E.D.N.Y. Feb. 20, 2004)

This case alleged systemic noncompliance by the New York state education agency, state social services agency, fifteen local educational agencies, and county social service agencies with state and federal laws, including the Act, relating to the education of homeless children. The school districts settled their portion of the case early in the proceedings, while the state and county social service agencies moved to dismiss the case. The court denied those motions to dismiss, holding the Act was enforceable. Ultimately, on August 31, 2005, all parties settled and agreed to comply with all applicable state and federal laws relating to homeless students. The court signed the settlement agreement and consent order on March 31, 2006.

The consent order mandated that New York State, amongst other things:

- Provide complete and timely information to homeless families about their rights under the McKinney-Vento Act, including the prominent placement of homeless rights posters and brochures in school administration offices, and the publication of the contact information of the New York State Technical and Education Assistance Center for Homeless Students.

- Provide appropriate and reasonable training to all school administrators who are likely to have contact with homeless children or their families about the education rights of homeless students.

- Make all reasonable efforts to ensure that homeless students receive transportation to and from school (including to before and after school activities and preschool programs that housed students are provided transportation).

- Revise and implement a dispute resolution process that recognizes the right of homeless students to immediate and continuing admission and transportation to school during the pendency of any dispute or appeal concerning admission or transportation.

For more information about this case and the subsequent consent decree, please contact the National Law Center at (202) 638-2535.

Bullock v. Bd. of Educ. of Montgomery Cnty., DKC-2002-798
(D. Md. Mar. 14, 2002)

Montgomery County is a large suburban school district bordering on Washington, D.C. A lawsuit and motion for temporary restraining order and preliminary injunction was filed against the county on behalf of several homeless families. The case raised many issues related to the Act, including the rights of children in transitional housing, "time limits" on homelessness for doubled-up families, and segregation. The court entered a permanent injunction on March 28, 2005, requiring the school board to interpret "school of origin" to include feeder schools, to allow homeless students to stay with their classmates as they matriculated from elementary to middle school or from middle to high school. The case eventually settled. The school district agreed to implement broad reforms ranging from giving children awaiting foster placement full rights under the Act to widely publicizing the rights of homeless children throughout the district, to training school administrators and school personnel on rights under the Act, to implementing new forms and school-based guidelines to identify and serve homeless children, to providing transportation to the school of origin within four school days of the request. The parties also agreed to a two-year monitoring period, and the school district further agreed to pay $195,000 in attorney fees to counsel for the plaintiff class.

Collier v. Bd. of Educ. of Prince George's Cnty., DKC-2001-1179
(D. Md. Sept. 10, 2001)

Prince George's County is a large suburban school district bordering on Washington, D.C. A class action lawsuit and a motion for temporary restraining order and preliminary injunction were filed against the school district, on behalf of homeless families in the county. Initially, the court ordered the school district to provide plaintiffs with transportation to their school of origin. The case was then expanded to include a broad range of issues under the Act, including transportation, identification, school selection, dispute resolution, and inter-agency issues. In September 2001, the case settled. The school district agreed to take broad reform measures to address all of these issues, including, but not limited to, providing informational outreach to homeless children and school personnel, upholding children's rights under the Act, establishing a toll free number for parents and children to contact with questions about their rights under the Act, and providing transportation and fee waivers. More than a thousand homeless school children have availed themselves of the new processes and procedures.

Lampkin v. District of Columbia, 886 F.Supp. 56 (D.D.C. 1995)

Ten parents, on behalf of their children, and the National Law Center on Homelessness & Poverty filed a lawsuit in federal court, challenging failure by DCPS to ensure free, appropriate education for children experiencing homelessness, as required by the Act. The suit alleged that DCPS was failing to: consider the best interests of children and youth in making school placements; ensure transportation to the schools that were in the students' best interests; coordinate social services and public education; and ensure comparable services and school meals for students experiencing homelessness. The trial court dismissed the suit, but the appeals court reversed, agreeing with the plaintiffs that the Act created enforceable rights, and remanded the case to the lower court. The trial court then issued an injunction, ordering DCPS to identify children experiencing homelessness and refer them for all services required by the law, including transportation, within 72 hours of a family's application for emergency shelter. For the children of the more than 300 families on the waiting list for emergency shelter, the court allowed two weeks. The court also ordered DCPS to provide tokens to all children and youth in homeless situations who had to travel more than 1.5 miles to school, and also to parents who chose to escort their children to school. DCPS was ordered to pay $185,000 in attorney fees and costs associated with the case. Subsequently, the District of Columbia withdrew from the Act's education program and moved the court to vacate the court's order. Citing the appeals court's statement that the Act was "sufficiently clear to put the States on notice of the obligations they assume when they choose to accept grants made under the Act," the trial court held that such withdrawal ended the obligation of DCPS provide assistance to homeless children under the Act and dissolved the injunction.

Salazar v. Edwards, 92 CH 5703 (Il. Cir. Ct. Cook Cnty.,
Settlement Agreement, July 27, 2000)

Litigation was filed in 1992 on behalf of two classes: homeless children and their parents residing in the City of Chicago) after the Chicago Public Schools (CPS) failed to meet the requirements of the McKinney Act and the Illinois Education of Homeless Children Act. After dismissal, appeal, and reinstatement in the trial court, an initial settlement was achieved. In

1999, following persistent noncompliance in several areas, plaintiffs filed a motion to enforce this settlement agreement. The court granted the motion, ordering full compliance with the settlement, a "massive informational campaign addressing the rights of the homeless throughout Chicago," trainings, designation of school personnel to ensure implementation of the settlement, data reporting, a court-appointed monitor, and sanctions of up to $1,000 per day for continued noncompliance. Plaintiffs also received an additional $189,000 in attorney fees. A subsequent comprehensive Settlement Agreement in July of 2000 dissolved the injunction and now currently governs the implementation of McKinney-Vento in Chicago including mandates for a homeless liaison in each school, immediate enrollment, transportation services, training, non-discrimination, tutoring services, notice, dispute processes, a mechanism for negotiation of and resolution of emergency and systemic problems and data production. Plaintiffs' counsel at the Law Project of the Chicago Coalition for the Homeless meets monthly with the lead staff in the CPS Students in Temporary Living Situations (STLS) program to ensure compliance, collaborate on new initiatives and ensure removal of barriers for all homeless students.

Residency Issues

A.E. v. Carlynton Sch. Dist., C.A. No. 09-1345 (W.D.P.A. 2009)

The Education Law Center-PA and the National Law Center on Homelessness & Poverty settled a lawsuit with the Pennsylvania Department of Education and the Carlynton School District, which ensured the continued enrollment of four homeless children in Allegheny County and significantly revised state polices to better protect the rights of homeless students. The suit began In October 2009, when Carlynton School District officials sought to remove four homeless children from a District school, claiming the family did not actually live in the District because while their day shelter was in the District, they spent nights in one of eight different locations, only some of which were in the District. When the Pennsylvania Department of Education concurred with the District's decision, the family sued under the Act. As part of the settlement agreement, the Pennsylvania Department of Education issued a new Basic Education Circular (BEC) that made clear that: (1) children, like the plaintiffs, who may sleep overnight in different places, are legally entitled to attend school where they have a substantial connection, including where they receive day shelter services, conduct daily living activities, or stay overnight on a recurring basis; and (2) school districts must immediately enroll a child who claims to be homeless and must notify families of their rights under the Act. Pennsylvania, in compliance with federal law, also now requires school districts to inform families in writing of the basis of a denial of school enrollment or school selection decision; apprise families of their right to remain in their school of choice pending resolution of a dispute; and explain the procedures for challenging a school district's decision.

This case is significant because it established state guidance regarding "highly mobile" students and their right to attend school where they have a "substantial connection" (e.g., daily living activities, day shelter, stay on recurring basis).

Muriel C. v. Gallagher (Il. Cir. Ct. Cook Cnty. Feb. 2003)

Muriel C. and her children lost their housing in Evergreen Park and then went to live with Muriel C.'s mother in Chicago, Illinois. In January 2003, the Chicago high school in that district issued the family letters stating that the children were to be excluded from school due to non-residency. The lawyer for the school district argued in a dispute resolution hearing—and the hearing officer agreed—that the family had the burden of proof to show that they were, in fact, homeless. Upon review, the hearing officer found that the family was not homeless and the children were excluded from the Chicago school for approximately two weeks. After the family filed a complaint in the Circuit Court of Cook County, with the assistance of the Law Project of the Chicago Coalition for the Homeless, the school district agreed to re-enroll the children.

Burgin v. Cmty. Conso. Sch. Dist. 168, Cook Cnty.
Comm'n on Human Rights (Nov. 22, 2000)

The Burgin family rented an apartment in District 168, and four of the children (two of whom were honor roll students) attended District 168 schools in Cook County, Illinois. In March of 2000, the Burgins were evicted from their apartment following a period of unemployment. They then went to live with family members in a nearby suburb. Thereafter the Burgins were denied continued enrollment in District 168 because they were not residents of that district. When an employee of the Illinois State Board of Education (ISBE) attempted to re-enroll the children, the superintendent stated: "If I let scum like that back in my schools, pretty soon the whole area will be a ghetto." After litigation was threatened, the District agreed to re-enroll. Because of the District's unlawful efforts to exclude the Burgin children even after being made aware of the legal requirements and because of the derogatory racial remark made about the family, the family filed a complaint with the Cook County Commission on Human Rights. The Cook County Human Rights Ordinance prohibits discrimination based on race as well as based on "housing status." Discovery was conducted in the case and revealed that all of the District's registration and enrollment materials and policy were misleading and inaccurate with respect to children experiencing homelessness. The parties entered into a settlement agreement in which the District agreed to, among other things: payment of a total monetary settlement of $100,000; conduct annual training on and implementation of the Act, the Illinois Education for Homeless Children Act and the Cook County Human Rights Ordinance; and establish a diverse committee of parents, staff, and community organizations to analyze the racial impact of school policies and practices.

No Time Limit on Homelessness

L.R. v. Steelton-Highspire Sch. Dist., C.A. No. 10-00468
(M.D. Pa., Mar. 2, 2010) (SHR)

In January 2009, a child, who resided with his grandmother, became homeless due to fire. The school the child was attending permitted him to continue attending school until the end of the school year, but refused to enroll him for the next school year. In March 2010, a homeless student and his grandmother, with the assistance of the Education Law Center and the National Law Center on Homelessness & Poverty, filed suit against the Steelton-Highspire School District in Pennsylvania, seeking damages and injunctive and declaratory relief requiring the defendants to comply with the Act. The court issued a preliminary injunction on March 29, 2010, and an opinion on the preliminary injunction on April 7, stating that: (1) homelessness has no time limit; (2) schools must follow dispute resolution procedures and immediately enroll students even if the schools do not believe they qualify as homeless; and (3) Congress had expressed its opinion in the Act that immediate enrollment pending disputes is in the public interest. On April 14, 2010, the court issued an order converting the preliminary injunction to a permanent injunction.

Rights of Students Displaced by Disasters

Boisseau v. Picard, Civil Action No. 2007-0565 (E.D. La. Feb. 1, 2007)

The NAACP Legal Defense Fund filed suit against Cecil Picard, Robin Jarvis, the Recovery School District, Phyllis Landrieu, the Orleans Parish School Board, and Linda Johnson to ensure that students who had been displaced by Hurricane Katrina would be able to enroll in school immediately when their families returned to New Orleans. Many returning students had been refused enrollment or placed on waiting lists. The parties settled the case with defendants agreeing to address the plaintiffs' concerns, including enrolling students by the second instructional day after they seek to become enrolled and providing a centralized application process for enrollment.

Cause of Homelessness is Irrelevant

Mitzi H. v. Murray and Bd. of Educ. of Homewood-Flossmoor High Sch. Dist. 233
Mitzi H. v. Ramsey and Bd. of Educ. of Homewood Sch. Dist. 153
(Il. Cir. Ct. Cook Cnty. Sept. 2002)

These two cases involved one family with two children in an elementary school district and one child in a high school district. Under the Act and Illinois law, when the children lost their housing in Homewood, they should have been permitted to stay in the Homewood schools and obtain transportation assistance. In fact, the children were kept out of school for a total of five months until shelter personnel in Chicago referred them to the Law Project. After advocacy by the Law Project of the Chicago Coalition for the Homeless, the students were re-enrolled in March 2002. In September 2002, two separate complaints were filed in the Circuit Court of Cook County against both the elementary and the high schools, seeking damages and other relief. The high school filed a motion to dismiss, arguing that the children could not bring suit because their homelessness was caused by a step-parent's wrongdoing. The high school also argued that the family was not homeless. After briefing and oral argument, the court denied the motion to dismiss. The court found that the Illinois statute protected children experiencing homelessness regardless of the reason for their homelessness. The court further found that the family met the definition of "homeless" when they were living in a motel. The parties engaged in settlement negotiations, but the details of the settlement have not been made public.

Supremacy of the McKinney-Vento Act

Doe v. Governor Wentworth Regional Sch. Dist. (Mar. 21, 2001)

After losing their housing in the fall of 2000, a family moved into a homeless shelter in a different school district. The parent sought to keep her children in their school of origin. However, conflicts between state laws and the Act resulted in a long dispute between the family and the school district of origin. The school district argued that the Act was not applicable because the district did not receive a sub-grant for homeless education programs and that the state could choose to force homeless children to attend school where they are temporarily residing. Despite active pre-litigation involvement by the State Coordinator and local attorneys, the school district refused to follow the law. Therefore, New Hampshire Legal Assistance filed an administrative complaint in March of 2001. On March 21, 2001, the Administrative Law Judge found in favor of the family. The children were permitted to remain in their school of origin.

Enrollment Issues

Doe v. Richardson, Civ. A. 98-1165-N (M.D. Ala. Oct. 13, 1998)

In October, 1998, the Southern Poverty Law Center brought a lawsuit again the state of Alabama and two school districts for violating the Act. The school district had adopted a policy requiring children to enroll in school within the first ten days of the semester. Anyone enrolling later, including homeless children, would only be admitted at the discretion of a special enrollment committee. A student residing at a shelter in the district was refused admission to the local high school, after she tried to enroll more than ten days after school had started. The local county board of education initially referred her to another high school, but that school had a tacit policy against enrolling African American students. After learning the student's race, the board offered to enroll her in a high school an hour away from the shelter. Overwhelmed by negative press, the state and school district agreed to settle the case immediately. The student was enrolled in the local high school, and the State Board of Education and both school districts adopted new policies affirming their duties under the Act and their commitment to nondiscrimination. The settlement also required defendants to pay $5,000 in attorney fees and costs associated with the case.

CHAPTER XIII

You Are Not Alone: Resources for Understanding and Implementing the McKinney-Vento Act

The American Bar Association (ABA), the National Association for the Education of Homeless Children and Youth (NAEHCY), the National Center for Homeless Education (NCHE), the National Law Center on Homelessness & Poverty (NLCHP), and the National Network for Youth (NN4Y) provide technical assistance, training, and educational resources related to implementing the McKinney-Vento Act. Key educational resources are highlighted below.

Basic McKinney-Vento Implementation

NAEHCY and NLCHP's "The Most Frequently Asked Questions on the Education of Children and Youth in Homeless Situations" provides concise answers, with legal citations, to over 100 questions asked frequently by schools and service providers.
http://naehcy.org/sites/default/files/images/dl/naehcy_faq.pdf

NAEHCY's Podcast Series – NAEHCY produces short monthly podcasts on a variety of topics.
http://naehcy.org/educational-resources/podcasts

NAEHCY's Awareness Videos – NAEHCY's video page contains links to YouTube and other videos on basic McKinney-Vento implementation and the role of homeless liaisons.
http://naehcy.org/educational-resources/videos

NCHE Issue Briefs – NCHE worked with NAEHCY and NLCHP to produce a wide range of issue briefs on the basic law and implementation of McKinney-Vento. Topics include transportation, enrollment, school selection, academic assessment, Title I Part A, and more.
http://center.serve.org/nche/pr/briefs.php

NCHE Directory – NCHE maintains a directory of all the state coordinators for the McKinney-Vento Act, as well as links to state data and state web pages.
http://center.serve.org/nche/states/state_resources.php

NCHE Posters – NCHE has produced posters on the basic educational rights of homeless children, and unaccompanied homeless youth. These posters may be downloaded, and are available in English and Spanish. **http://center.serve.org/nche/pr/er_poster.php#parent**

NCHE Online Training – NCHE offers online training that is either self-paced, or live and interactive. Topics range from basic McKinney-Vento Issues to determining eligibility and Title I. **http://center.serve.org/nche/web/online_tr.php**

NCHE Helpline – NCHE provides a toll-free helpline and email to respond to questions from schools, service providers, parents, and youth. **http://center.serve.org/nche/helpline.php**

Early Childhood Education

NAEHCY's Early Childhood Education page contains a summary of homelessness-related provisions in federal early childhood programs, sample school district pre-school plans, and links to federal guidance for child care and Head Start programs. **http://naehcy.org/educational-resources/early-childhood**

NCHE's Preschool/Early Childhood page contains an issue brief on homelessness and early childhood, as well as links to other research and resource documents. **http://center.serve.org/nche/ibt/sc_preschool.php**

Displaced Students

NCHE's disaster response and preparation page contains issue briefs, handbooks, and a toolbox for helping school districts and relief agencies meet the educational needs of children and youth who have been displaced by disasters. **http://center.serve.org/nche/ibt/dis_prep.php**

Food and Nutrition

NAEHCY's food and nutrition page contains links to federal guidance and memos on homelessness, school meals, and the Supplemental Nutrition Assistance Program (SNAP), as well as an issue brief on improving access to food assistance for homeless children. **http://naehcy.org/educational-resources/food**

Foster Care

The ABA's Legal Center for Foster Care and Education contains issue briefs, fact sheets, and many other tools and training resources on the education of children and youth in foster care. **http://www.american-bar.org/groups/child_law/what_we_do/projects/education.html**

Higher Education/Financial Aid

NAEHCY's higher education page contains a toolkit on college access for educators and service providers, FAFSA tips for unaccompanied youth, a template for FAFSA determinations, and many other tools and resources. **http://naehcy.org/educational-resources/higher-ed**

NCHE's Higher Education page contains issue briefs, tools, posters, and links to federal guidance on homelessness and financial aid. **http://center.serve.org/nche/ibt/higher_ed.php**

Unaccompanied Youth

ABA Commission on Homelessness & Poverty's Homeless Youth and the Law Initiative features advocacy resources such as "Runaway and Homeless Youth and the Law: Model State Statutes" and free technical assistance and training for educators, lawyers, and advocates. **http://www.ambar.org/homeless**

NAEHCY's unaccompanied homeless youth page contains a toolkit for counselors, service providers, and financial aid administrators; a report on how to create housing for homeless youth; a report on undocumented unaccompanied homeless youth; and many other resources. **http://naehcy.org/educational-resources/youth**

NLCHP and NN4Youth's report, "Alone Without a Home: A State-by-State Review of Laws Affecting Unaccompanied Homeless Youth," reviews state laws on unaccompanied homeless youth in many areas, including health, education, income, and shelter. **http://www.nlchp.org/Alone_Without_A_Home**

Technical Assistance and Training

For information about technical assistance and CLE training, please contact the ABA Commission on Homelessness & Poverty at (202) 662-1693 or **homeless@americanbar.org.**

NAEHCY convenes the only annual national conference on the education of children and youth experiencing homelessness. Information is available at **www.naehcy.org/conference/conference**. NCHE offers a variety of free webinars every month, as well as self-paced training and technical assistance. Training information is available at **center.serve.org/nche/web/online_tr.php,** and the toll-free technical assistance hotline is (800) 308-2145.

Endnotes

1 The Stewart B. McKinney Homeless Assistance Act, Pub. L. No. 100-77, § 721(1), 101 Stat. 482, 525 (1987). The complete text of the Act is available at http://center.serve.org/nche/downloads/mv-full-text.docx.

2 Report to the President and Congress on the Implementation of the Education for Homeless Children and Youth Program Under the McKinney-Vento Homeless Assistance Act, U.S. Department of Education, March 2006.

3 U.S. Department of Education, Federal Data Collection 2011-2012.

4 Id. It is important to note that this number is not an estimate of the prevalence of child and youth homelessness. It is an underestimate, since not all school districts reported data, and the data collected represents only those children identified and enrolled in school. Finally, the number does not include preschool children.

5 Burt, Aron, Douglas, et al., Homelessness: Programs and the People They Serve: Summary Report-Findings of the National Survey of Homeless Assistance Providers and Clients, The Urban Institute (1999).

6 National Low Income Housing Coalition, Out of Reach (2009), at http://nlihc.org/oor/2009/.

7 Harvard University, Joint Center for Housing Studies, The State of the Nation's Housing (2013), at http://www.jchs.harvard.edu/sites/jchs.harvard.edu/files/son2013.pdf.

8 MVC.U.S. Conference of Mayors, A Status Report on Hunger and Homelessness in America's Cities (2013).

9 Toro, P., Dworsky, A. and Fowler, P. (2007). "Homeless Youth in the United States: Recent Research Findings and Intervention Approaches." Toward Understanding Homelessness: The 2007 National Symposium on Homelessness Research. Washington DC: U.S. Dept. of Housing and Urban Development.; National Runaway Switchboard, http://www.1800runaway.org/.

10 See Report, Institute for Children, Poverty & Homelessness, "An Unstable Foundation: Factors that Impact Educational Attainment among Homeless Children," http://www.icphusa.org/index.asp?page=16&report=116&pg=122

11 See http://www.usich.gov/usich_resources/fact_sheets/opening_doors_homelessness_among_families_fact_sheet .

12 U.S. Conference of Mayors, A Status Report on Hunger and Homelessness in America's Cities (2006).

13 U.S. Department of Education. Federal Data Collection 2011-2012.

14 Audette, R., Algozzine, R., & Warden, M., Mobility and student achievement, PSYCHOL. REP., 701, 701–02 (1993). Benson, G. P., Haycraft, J. L., Steyaert, J. P., & Weigel, D. J., Mobility in sixth graders as related to achievement, adjustment, and socioeconomic status, 16 PSYCHOL. IN THE SCH. 444, 444–47 (1979). Mao, M. X., Whitset, M. D., & Mellor, L. T., Student mobility, academic performance, and school accountability (Report No. TM 026 966). Austin, TX: (ERIC Document Reproduction Service No. ED409380) (1997). Rumberger, R. W., Larson, K. A. Student mobility and increased risk of high school dropout, 107 AM. J. of EDUC. 1, 1-35 (1998). Rumberger, R.W., Larson, K. A., Ream, R. K., & Polardy, G.J., The educational consequences of mobility for California students and schools (No.1, Vol. 1). Berkeley, CA: University of California.

15 Dr. Joy Rogers of the Loyola University Department of Education, Education Report of Rule 706 Expert Panel presented in B.H. v. Johnson, 715 F. Supp. 1387 (N.D. Ill. 1989), 1991.

16 Del Stover, Schools Grapple with High Student Mobility Rates, 20 Sch. Board News 11 (June 13, 2000).

17 U.S. Department of Education, Report to the President and Congress on the Implementation of the Education for Homeless Children and Youth Program Under the McKinney-Vento Homeless Assistance Act (March 2006).

18 Carlson, D., Reder, S., Jones, N., Lee, A. Homeless Student Transportation Project Evaluation. (2006). Seattle: Washington State Transportation Center.

19 Under the Act, six specific segregated schools in Arizona and California are permitted to continue operation subject to a series of new and stringent mandates. Those mandates are beyond the scope of this book.

20 U.S. Department of Health and Human Services, Administration for Children and Families; Administration on Children, Youth and Families; Head Start Bureau, Serving Homeless Families: Descriptions, Effective Practices, and Lessons Learned (April 1999).

21 See Report, "Homeless Children: Update on Research, Policy, Programs, and Opportunities" at http://aspe.hhs.gov/hsp/10/homelesschildrenroundtable/index.shtml, May 2010.

22 Burt, Aron, Douglas, et al., Homelessness: Programs and the People They Serve: Summary Report-Findings of the National Survey of Homeless Assistance Providers and Clients (Washington, DC: The Urban Institute, 1999).

23 Barnett Ph.D, Steven W.; Carolan, Megan E. M.P.P.; Fitzgerald, Jen MLIS & Squires, James H. Ph.D. The State of Preschool 2012, p. 6, The National Institute for Early Education Research, Rutgers University Graduate School of Education (2012) found at http://nieer.org/sites/nieer/files/yearbook2012.pdf.

24 Id.

25 Id.

26 Tex. Ed. Code 29.153.

27 See Report, Community Organizing and Family Issues COFI, "Why Isn't Johnny in Preschool" http://www.cofionline.org/files/earlylearningreport.pdf, May 29, 2009.

28 The amendments related to homelessness in the 2007 Head Start Act reauthorization were extensive. For a complete summary of all homeless-related Head Start amendments, please see http://www.naehcy.org/educational-resources/early-childhood.

29 As of this writing (January 2014), these regulations had not been issued.

30 States also have the option to provide services to infants and toddlers who are at risk of a developmental delay, although only six states do so: California, Hawaii, Massachusetts, New Hampshire, New Mexico, and West Virginia. Jo Shackelford (2006). State and Jurisdictional Eligibility Definitions for Infants and Toddlers with Disabilities Under IDEA. Chapel Hill NC: National Early Childhood Technical Assistance Center. Accessed June 30, 2007, at http://www.nectac.org/~pdfs/pubs/nnotes21.pdf.

31 20 U.S.C. §1435; 34 C.F.R. 303.301(b).

32 Currently, all states participate in IDEA Part C. If a state chooses not to participate, it will not be bound by these requirements.

33 See, e.g., Michael G. MacLean, Lara E. Embry, and Ana Mari Cauce, Homeless Adolescents' Paths to Separation from Family: Comparison of Family Characteristics, Psychological Adjustment and Victimization, 27 J.OF COMMUNITY PSYCH. 179, 179-87 (1999).

34 National Working Group on Foster Care and Education. (2011) Education is the Lifeline for Youth in Foster Care. http://www.fostercareandeducation.org/Database.aspx?EntryId=1279&Command=Core_Download&method=inline.

35 The AFCARS Report #14: Preliminary 2006 Estimates as of Jan 2008, U.S. Department of Health and Human Services, Administration for Children and Families, Administration on Children, Youth and Families, Children's Bureau, http://www.acf.hhs.gov/programs/cb/stats_research/afcars/tar/report14.htm

36 Id.

37 Id.

38 Child Welfare Outcomes 2002-2005: Report to Congress, Chapter IV, U.S. Department of Health and Human Services, Administration for Children and Families, Child Welfare Outcomes 2002-2005: Report to Congress, Chapter IV, September, 2008, at http://www.acf.hhs.gov/programs/cb/pubs/cwo05/chapters/chapter4.htm

39 Courtney, M.E., Terao, S. & Bost, N. (2004). Midwest evaluation of the adult functioning of former foster youth: Conditions of youth preparing to leave state care. Chapin Hall working paper. Chicago, IL: Chapin Hall Center for Children at the University of Chicago. Wave One of Longitudinal study in three waves following 732 youth age 17 or 18 still in jurisdiction in Illinois, Iowa and Wisconsin as they age out of foster care. Youth were also compared to 19 years olds who were part of the National Longitudinal Study of Adolescent Health, as a comparison national sample.

40 Id.

41 Legal Center for Foster Care and Education. (2013) State-by-State School Stability Chart. http://www.fostercareandeducation.org/Database.aspx?EntryId=1861&Command=Core_Download&method=inline.

42 For information about IDEA Part C, the Infant Toddler Early Intervention Program, refer to Chapter V, Young Children Without Homes: Creating Access to Early Childhood Education Opportunities through Three Federal Laws.

43 Better Homes Fund, Homeless children: America's new outcasts (1999).

44 The Individuals with Disabilities Education Act, 20 U.S.C. §§1400 et seq.

45 34 C.F.R. Part 300.

46 The regulations define "include" to mean "that the items named are not all the possible items that are covered, whether like or unlike the ones named."

47 The term "ward" is defined in IDEA statute at 20 U.S.C. § 1201(36).

48 20 U.S.C. § 6301.

49 Under the Family Educational Rights and Privacy Act (FERPA), schools may disclose educational records for financial aid purposes without parental consent. 34 C.F.R. §99.31(4). This includes verifying that a youth is homeless and unaccompanied.